Deterrence and Strategy

Deterrence and Strategy

by

Général d'Armée André Beaufre

translated from the French

by

Major-General R. H. Barry C.B., C.B.E.

FABER AND FABER
24 Russell Square
London

First published in England in mcmlxv
by Faber and Faber Limited
24 Russell Square London WC1
Printed in Great Britain
by Ebenezer Baylis & Son, Limited
The Trinity Press, Worcester, and London
All rights reserved

First published in France by Armand Colin
under the title Dissuasion et Stratégie

To

CAPTAIN B. H. LIDDELL HART
who has contributed so greatly
to the revival of strategy

Contents

CONTENTS

PART TWO

THE CONSEQUENCES OF DETERRENCE

8

DIAGRAMS

SKETCH MAPS

Foreword

Ever since 1945 – since Hiroshima in other words – there has been a loss of confidence in the efficacy of a defence effort. Our 1940 defeat sowed the seeds of doubt; that doubt was substantiated by fifteen years of fruitless overseas struggles and increased by the overwhelming and apparently inexplicable novelty of the nuclear weapon; the result has been a vague feeling that the burden of national defence has its roots in obsolete traditions. Unable to understand the new rules, in any case too contradictory, too conjectural and too fluid to carry conviction, we have been driven to take refuge at one time in the great illusion of disarmament and at another in the abdication of our responsibilities, handing over the security of Europe to the United States. Our young people have already forgotten Hitler and are tempted to turn their attention to problems of an entirely different nature. The armies of the West have been bled by anti-guerilla campaigns, the French worst of all in Indo-China and Algeria but the British have had to cope with Kenya, Cyprus and Malaya and the Americans are now learning their lesson in Vietnam; armies are therefore going through a period of mental turmoil and are in danger of losing all sense of purpose in their day to day business.

This disillusionment is a most serious matter; thanks to the nuclear weapon, peace in Europe is at present passing through a period of exceptional stability but that stability must not blind us to the fact that there are formidable developments in the background: there are dark clouds on the horizon of the future.

The great problem of our era is not simply how to harmonize the powerful resources provided by science and modern technology with the civilization compounded of Greco-Latin and Christian traditions which Europe has contrived to construct. This emergent civilization will be that of the third millennium; it must be defended against the growing dangers of a shrinking and over-populated world. The defence function is no less important than the creative. The two are complementary. It is therefore vital to re-establish our belief in the function of defence and our confidence in the means of fulfilling it.

This is a problem which has been worrying me for many years; I have come to the conclusion that the only method of solving it is to reach an understanding of the profound changes which have taken place in the interplay of the use of force as a factor in relationships between nations or groups of nations. Only by this method can we recover the conviction we now lack and the efficiency which would support and reinforce that conviction. Pursuing this line of thought, I believe that strategy constitutes the only effective method of explaining this phenomenon.

In my previous book, *Introduction to Strategy*, I attempted to classify and define the concepts on which strategy is based. Now, taking as a starting point the overriding phenomenon of deterrence, my object is to bring out the reasoning behind the main conclusions which can be deduced therefrom. This is an ambitious undertaking and I cannot hope to do more than give certain indications of the processes of strategic thinking.

In the meanwhile certain solutions have been put forward in France giving rise to sometimes heated debate both nationally and internationally.

This book does not pretend to provide a complete answer to the questions of the day, questions generally discussed on the basis of inadequate data and against a political rather than a strategic background. My present object is exactly the opposite: to set out objectively the strategic principles which may help to clarify the debate. Nevertheless the whole debate inevitably includes a highly important political element which is outside the field of strategy and therefore of the present treatise. I shall of course be forced to point out certain political results which strategy would *recommend* but cannot dictate; there can be no greater error than to base a policy solely upon strategic requirements. The end must be the decisive factor not the means.

Finally I would warn my readers against an understandable but dangerous reaction. All human phenomena are a compound of mind and matter, of emotion and calculation. The effort of trying to deal with these problems from an unemotional and rational standpoint must never lead us to forget the irrational element, sometimes base, sometimes sublime. Equally, however, this factor must not be allowed to outweigh reason. Apart from their victory in 1945, the democracies have suffered a series of uninterrupted defeats over a period of thirty years and so it is our duty to lay the bones of the problem bare in order to discover the fundamental background to our unhappy experiences. There have been all sorts of reasons, many of them having nothing to do with strategy but the central feature has been the fact that strategic thought has fallen into disuetude and we have misjudged the true nature of the phenomena in which we are involved.

If we wish, in the current phrase, to get off to a good start, we must first *understand* the new world which is growing up around us; then we shall be able to diagnose the situation objectively and see what actions will be the most effective in attaining whatever object we may have set ourselves. Only if we can regain this efficiency have we any right to make a new appeal for enthusiasm and the acceptance of sacrifices, hitherto made generously but all too often blindly and uselessly.

If we can do this it is my hope that the popular attitude to defence will regain balance and armed forces their true *raison d'être*.

Introduction

Looked at from a distance, nuclear strategy presents an imposing skyline rather like that seen by the traveller as he approaches New York. The nearer you get to it, however, the more you realize that although the whole may be made up of a large number of magnificent skyscrapers, they frequently bear little or no relation to each other. Worse still, many of them are not the product of a consistent train of thought but the synthetic result of numerous readjustments and sometimes even of the introduction of irrelevant side issues. The deeper one digs down into the labyrinth of theory, the more one is struck by the succession of contradictory illusions; one is frequently brought up short by obvious distortion introduced by politics and the heady interests of the arms industries.

The fact is that nuclear strategy has been built up in the fever of a ferment of ideas but in considerable confusion and by a succession of empirical developments, almost invariably aimed at solving the specific problems posed at any one moment by some evolution in the armament of the two contestants. At each stage the intellectual structure has become more complicated and undergone such transmutation that on several occasions it has changed its very nature: during the initial period efforts were directed primarily to maintaining and increasing the destructive and penetrative capability of the initial strike; then people concentrated on producing methods of reducing the effect of the enemy's initial strike; finally we have reached the present situation when each side is doing its best to extract the maximum deterrent effect from the fact that in both camps a sizeable proportion of the forces involved is practically invulnerable. Over-simplifying somewhat, it is true to say that attention has been concentrated in turn upon three different aspects thrown up by three different situations: first offensive, then defensive, finally relative parity. Put in yet another way and even more precisely, the primary preoccupation of the Americans has throughout been to retain the initiative but in order to maintain their offensive capability they have had to adapt their methods to the evolution in the relative balance of forces; this they have done first thanks to their undisputed superiority, then in spite of an increasing enemy reaction capability and finally in spite of the achievement of a sort of equilibrium.

Today all these succeeding theories still exist more or less side by side depending on the degree of understanding reached by their protagonists of a phenomenon which theory and material progress has made more and more complex. There is therefore an increasing diversity of opinion expressed by the 'experts'; moreover, in spite of reasoning and even mathematical analysis, these 'experts' are often the spokesmen of emotional or political points of view rather than of really objective ideas.

Is it possible to cut through all this and to find criteria enabling us to put some order into the present day confusion? This is what I propose to try to do, not in order to support any particular theory but to see whether a choice between the various current theories can be made on the basis of adequately convincing argument.

Last year I produced *Introduction to Strategy*; this was not, nor was it intended to be, more than an 'Introduction'; it aimed only to delimit the concept of strategy and to set out its essential sub-divisions and methods. It was therefore simply a preliminary 'clearing of the ground'; its object was to prove that strategy can never be some homogeneous doctrine but is in fact the art of making the best choice from among various possible doctrines and procedures and selecting those best fitted to the case concerned.

In this overall study I naturally dealt with the main problems of present day strategy, nuclear strategy and indirect strategy; but I did not try to do more than give a general idea of them and made no attempt really to solve any of their problems.

The present study is quite different in nature: it is intended to be a study in depth, concentrated upon an object, limited perhaps, but vital in view of its importance in the present-day world, the *strategy of deterrence*.

In the previous book I did no more than sketch out the broad lines of this strategy; but it is in fact the decisive component of nuclear strategy which itself is the keystone of contemporary military structure. No explanation of the present day strategic situation can be satisfactory without definition of the nuclear situation and no definition of the nuclear situation is possible without thorough knowledge of the laws governing deterrence.

Though many books and treatises have been written on this subject, they tend to contain flat statements rather than proof, contradictions – or even polemics – rather than established facts: in some people's view the qualitative aspect of nuclear weapons is such that a small number of them is enough to produce deterrence; in other people's view a complete and highly diversified nuclear system is absolutely essential; one school of thought will only envisage a bipolar (American and Russian) world system; in the view of another school all countries should try to provide themselves with nuclear weapons, however few in number; finally the supporters of counter-force tactics question the necessity of too powerful nuclear weapons, whereas the supporters of counter-city tactics are the protagonists of a weapon with the greatest possible destructive power. Added to all these conflicting theories is the debate on the role of tactical nuclear weapons and conventional armaments. One is accordingly driven to the conclusion that it is essential to clarify our ideas in order to arrive, if possible, at established facts, essential if any rational total strategy and any suitable military system are to be worked out.

This is the object which I have set myself in this book and it is an ambitious one; I shall try to achieve it in two stages.

In Part One, by a process of basic analysis of the phenomenon I shall try to uncover the laws of deterrence. The essence of this analysis is to a large extent the result of studies produced and discussed during 1963–64 in the Institut Français d'Études Stratégiques.

Convinced that fundamental research was essential, we were led to work out empirically a method of examination both sufficiently flexible to take account of the maximum number of factors and sufficiently precise to arrive at firmly based conclusions. Discussion of the various solutions put forward proved extremely productive of ideas and I sincerely believe that the results achieved deserve some consideration, although naturally I do not pretend that they deal with the subject exhaustively.

As the reader will see, the essential feature of our method has been to deal first with the most simple problem, that of bilateral deterrence between two 'great powers'; at this stage our object was to discover and isolate the various levels at which force can be employed, to analyse the laws of deterrence peculiar to each level and to set out the deterrent effect which the various levels exert upon each other. Having thus got clear the various ideas on bilateral deterrence, we then studied the influence on this deterrence of a third party, noticeably less powerful than the two principals; we then extrapolated the results, applying them to a situation in which a larger number of nuclear powers existed. This logical procedure, starting from the simple case and moving on to the more complicated, has been set out at more or less regular intervals in a number of exposés published in our Review, *Stratégie*; but although convincing, they are somewhat strong meat for the non-specialist. It therefore seemed advisable to produce a book less closely argued from the point of view of proving the case but easier to read. From time to time, in order to prove a point, I shall refer to our basic study, but in order not to overload the book, the object of which is to explain rather than to prove, I shall do this only in the case of the more important sections.

In Part Two, we shall try to deduce the effects of the laws of deterrence on the general concept of contemporary strategy and military structure.

My primary object in Part Two has been to see whether there is some objective strategic truth which remains unaffected by any consideration of particular situations. This is an essential step, since not only is the problem of deterrence complex in itself, but it has highly delicate political aspects, resulting from the French initiative for the formation of an independent deterrent force and from the opposition to that initiative, particularly on the part of the United States.

As we shall see, it is perfectly possible to produce strategic arguments, but without launching into a discussion on the choice of the political objectives governing strategy, these arguments do not in general lead to firm conclusions on the strategic problems now facing us. The present study therefore makes no attempt to answer the questions raised by the 'great debate', for in essence that debate is political. On the other hand, by setting out the strategic logic linking ends to means, we may be able to bring some clarification to the political debate. The reader will therefore find that arguments are sometimes put forward which support certain of the most debatable tendencies of present day French policy; sometimes on the other hand the arguments advanced will seem far removed from anything generally considered as orthodox. In both cases they will be the result of a process of thought which has been kept as objective as possible and is inspired solely by the desire to reach the most rational solutions.

But the further one goes in the study of deterrence, the clearer it becomes that we are faced with an entirely new phenomenon, new both in its scope, in its trends and in its procedures. It has always been necessary to counter aggression but the necessity to counter the outbreak of any form of war is a problem peculiar to modern times. Ever since 1918 we have tried to achieve this object by a variety of methods, all of which have failed in turn. The appearance of the nuclear weapon, initially considered an evil thing, provides us with an unexpected solution, for it is emerging more and more as the most powerful stabilizer man has ever known since the dawn of time. Naturally it is still not one hundred per cent effective; the nuclear weapon cannot stop up all the little cracks through which seep the more insidious forms of action used by indirect strategy. Naturally too, the risk of nuclear conflict still remains; conversely there remains the risk of nuclear deterrence cancelling itself out; both these factors leave a nagging doubt hanging over our state of comparative peace.

But the most striking discovery to which study of deterrence leads is that it is the risk of nuclear conflict which keeps the peace so stable. This essential contradiction between the magnitude of the danger and the beneficent effect of its risk is one of the essential characteristics of our era, an era so new from many points of view. We stumble here upon an unexpected truth which may help us to disentangle the underlying nature of that technical world which lies in the womb of our civilization.

Part One

The Laws of Deterrence

One

Deterrence the Key to Contemporary Strategy

THE IMPORTANCE OF DETERRENCE

To find our way through the complicated maze of arguments and opinions on contemporary strategy, we must go back to the central concept; otherwise we shall merely add to the tangle, already complicated enough.

In my short book *Introduction to Strategy* I attempted to set out and clarify the concept of strategy and its main component elements. Starting from this basis, I have looked to see what is the decisive factor; with this as a background, our reasoning can follow the logical and therefore the simplest sequence.

Today, this decisive factor is incontestably *deterrence*. The idea is not, of course, new (it runs from the 'si vis pacem para bellum' and the 'limes' of the Romans to the Maginot Line and Lyautey's phrase about 'making a show of force in order not to have to use it'). The term, however, is new, bearing witness to an attitude of mind quite different from that of the past and clearly the product of the existence of nuclear weapons.

In fact the old (pre-nuclear) strategy rested more or less explicitly upon a positive capability, the capacity to win; in other words not merely to impose one's will upon the enemy but to do so at relatively little cost to oneself, as compared to the fruits of victory. With the advent of the nuclear weapon, an entirely new phenomenon appears: whatever may be the outcome of the struggle, both victor and vanquished (assuming this distinction can still be drawn) must pay

23

the exorbitant price exacted by nuclear destruction *because there is no effective defence*; as a result, people now seek to achieve their political objectives, not by military victory, a positive capacity now too dangerous, but by indirect action, the object of which is to paralyse the enemy; this is achieved through a negative capability avoiding the great trial of strength, in other words through 'deterrence'. Naturally the enemy's paralysis is seldom total and it is then necessary to use other methods to exploit his partial paralysis; nevertheless, deterrence casts its shadow over the whole field of strategy and dictates both its limits and its form. Deterrence has therefore indeed become the key to contemporary strategy.

Deterrence is in the first place expected to preserve the peace and maintain the territorial status quo; but it is also expected to stop this or that action by the enemy, to limit the extent and intensity of conflict, and even in some cases to paralyse all enemy resistance to some action it is proposed to take. So herculean a role for deterrence, ranging from purposes entirely defensive in nature right through to its employment in aid of basically offensive action, necessitates as precise as possible a realization and delimitation of the true potentialities of deterrence; in so vital a field, hasty or approximate estimates will not do.

Our analysis must therefore be meticulous and thorough.

DEFINITION OF DETERRENCE

We must begin by analysing the notion of deterrence.

The object of deterrence is to *prevent* an enemy power *taking the decision* to use armed force; put in more general terms this means compelling him, when faced with a given situation, to act or react in the light of the *existence* of a set of dispositions which constitute an effective threat. The result which it is desired to achieve is therefore a psychological one and it is sought by means of a threat.[1]

This psychological result is the product of the combined effect of a *calculation* of the risk incurred compared to the issue at stake and

---

[1] The way in which deterrence acts is basically the exact opposite of that of war, in that the object of deterrence is to *prevent* the enemy taking a decision to act, whereas the object of war is to *force him* to take the decision to accept the conditions it is desired to impose on him.

of the *fear* engendered by the risks and uncertainties of conflict. The calculation is based upon a study of material data. The fear springs from complex psychological factors of a political, social, moral, etc. nature. These factors are frequently closely linked to the material calculation but, on occasions, may be independent of it.

Material data and psychological factors are therefore two complementary aspects of deterrence. I propose to examine the various facets of the problem of deterrence in this order.

The notion of deterrence can be split down into numerous categories depending upon its scope and on the methods employed to achieve it. Present day strategic literature has produced an entire vocabulary, highly complex and frequently chaotic;[1] but it can be reduced to the following:

If deterrence is used simply to prevent an enemy initiating against one an action of which one is afraid, its effect is *defensive*; if on the other hand it is used to prevent the enemy resisting some action which one proposes to take oneself, deterrence is *offensive*:

This offensive or defensive action may be either direct or indirect, depending upon its use either between two opponents or for the benefit of a third party:

Finally, deterrence may be *total* if it is applicable to all shades of the use of force or *limited* if it applies to a portion of the spectrum only. But as soon as it is no longer total – as is generally the case – it becomes necessary to define its precise scope. This opens up a most delicate analysis; it will lead us to dissect a vital concept, that of the existence of differing *levels* of the use of force.

LEVELS OF USE OF FORCE

The old-time levels

In the not too distant past – say prior to 1914 – we were still in the age of the two-tier strategic system: the political struggle on the one

---

[1] Deterrence has been categorized as active, passive, offensive, defensive, direct, indirect, total, relative, absolute, finite, positive, negative, deterrence of supremacy, type 1, 2, 3, and so on.

hand and the traditional military struggle on the other. We called the first *peace* and the second *war*. The main features of war were the suspension of the peacetime rules of jurisprudence and the institution of a special code permitting the use of violence against a named enemy; even in most primitive civilizations, however, this code included a whole list of limitations: war always gave one the right to kill or capture one's enemy but, depending on the circumstances, one could or one could not, for instance, take possession of his goods, maltreat or even torture him, destroy his family, etc. Peace, on the other hand, was characterized by a return to the juridical rules normal between human societies or states. During this period, although wars may have appeared terrible to those who lived at the time, they were considered natural phenomena, 'the pursuit of policy by other means' in Clausewitz' phrase; they therefore constituted one of the methods of conducting international politics.

The basic reasons for this attitude towards war are complex. Sociologists have ascribed it to the persistence of primitive instincts (the legend of Cain), to a throw-back to the ancient festal virility rites [*sic*] and a desire to escape from the constraints of civilization, or to a re-awakening of the taste for adventure and plunder. Undoubtedly wars signified a return to a mode of life rooted in the habits of our forbears of the distant past. To these motivations of a psychological nature, the strategists would add certain more material reasons: war was undoubtedly hard for the combatants, pitiless for the vanquished, but extremely profitable for the victor. War was 'a paying proposition'. As soon as there was sufficient expectation of success, war, the judgment of God, appeared to be the most suitable method of resolving conflicts. The fortunes of war were so uncertain that more often than not both sides thought their chances of success sufficient to justify risking the adventure. Even in periods when the risks implicit in defeat were enormous, as in ancient times, a sort of psychological aberration called 'military adventurism' by the Marxists, caused people to accept the risk with little hesitation. But in most cases the rules of war meant that the risks were in fact relatively limited: the taboos at first, then the Church and finally civilization so humanized war that in the light of the savage habits of the time it appeared not only possible but even, on occasions, attractive. The ease with which people resorted to war over minor incidents (the Ems telegram, the Algiers fan, the assassination of an Archduke, etc.) carried with it a considerable and valuable compensation: peacetime pressures were necessarily very restricted. The political struggle remained confined within extremely narrow limits. Peace was unstable but it was real peace.

On the other hand when war was let loose, hostilities might take place at any level of violence, ranging from mere skirmishes to a war of attrition and extermination, called by Clausewitz, who had seen its archetype in the Napoleonic period, 'escalation to the limit'. The political conduct of war consisted merely of proportioning the degree of force used to the magnitude of the stake, but escalation was gradual and there were no very clearly defined thresholds. For this reason, in spite of its diversity, war was conducted on a single level only.

What made war a tolerable phenomenon was that in general it was either decisive–and so advantageous for the victor–or very limited in its effects and settled by a compromise implying no slur upon the honour of the combatants. In other words war was a game in which, if you did not win straight away, you normally tried to reduce your stake. Nevertheless, at certain periods of evolution, when military operations were indecisive[1] and in the case of conflicts too savage to permit true compromise (the Hundred Years War, for instance), war was interminable. Though conducted at a low level of intensity, the damage it produced was fearful. People emerged from these prolonged wars exhausted, dazed and inoculated for some time to come against their bellicose tendencies. After such periods (the Thirty Years War, for instance), policies became more peaceful and wars more limited, both in their objectives and their intensity. Then would come another generation, technical development revived the possibility of rapid decision by military means, and war, glorified by legend, regained its old appeal.

The influence of industrial warfare

In the see-saw of the history of war, increasingly dangerous changes

[1] See *Introduction to Strategy*, Chapter II, 'Traditional Military Strategy'.

have appeared, each heralding a new phase: the Napoleonic whirl-wind left Europe dazzled but determined to prevent the recurrence of crises of such magnitude; the American Civil War, the first great war of modern times, passed almost unnoticed by Europe but was the precursor of the 1914-18 drama.

This shows at once that some new thing has in each case appeared to change completely the traditional character of warfare. The most obvious point today is the military impotence of position warfare, a specialized form of a cyclic but always unexpected phenomenon.[1] But it is also clear that what made war intolerable was the magnitude of the destruction it produced due to the vast numbers employed and the increasingly powerful armaments with which armed forces were equipped. Now the reasons for this change of scale were in the first place industrialization, which enabled weapons to be produced cheaply and in abundance; secondly the railways and then motor transport, enabling masses of armed men in numbers approaching the total available male population of military age, to be moved and supplied. War emerged from the age of the craftsman and the peasant, and entered upon that rightly called by Stalin 'the manu-facturing age'; it is this which made war intolerable. Since, in addition, thinking on war was dominated by pseudo-Clausewitzian concepts of war *à outrance* the traditional notion of compromise was forgotten, the catastrophe reached its paroxysm and Europe in-flicted grave wounds upon itself.

Popular instinct moreover, profoundly changed by the social influences of the machine age, did not err: in its view this war should have been the last. It was not, because twenty years later a new generation had partially forgotten the lessons of battle, also because Hitler thought that he was still living in the nineteenth century and because he was encouraged by the timidity of allied reaction, a timidity, be it noted, which to a large extent sprang from a more accurate appreciation than Hitler's of the potentialities of modern warfare.

The war of 1939-45 simply reproduced on a larger scale the characteristics of that of 1914-18. This time the phenomenon of position warfare was no longer present to conceal the new truth:

[1] See *Introduction to Strategy*, Chapter II, 'Traditional Military Strategy'.

warfare in the manufacturing age with its masses of men, its lethal machines, its exhausting industrial effort, its expansion to a world-wide scale and its ideological paroxysm had in fact become an absurd cataclysm. It was no longer conceivable as a normal means of conducting international politics.

Nevertheless, the resulting disturbances of the world balance created dangerous political tensions, aggravated by the setback to civilization brought about by this fearful war. Were men going to go on fighting among the ruins, stupefied and exhausted though they were?

The influence of the nuclear weapon

At this point came the Hiroshima and Nagasaki bombs putting an end to the age of manufacturing warfare and opening the age of scientific-technical warfare.

But nature does not proceed by leaps and bounds. For fifteen years people continued to believe that the old characteristics of warfare would persist, though intensified considerably by nuclear weapons. Then gradually a new truth emerged, though still not fully grasped. The enormous scale of destruction of which we had now become capable, not only by the use of nuclear weapons, but also through chemical and bacteriological warfare, all three poisoned fruits of scientific effort, meant that this type of warfare was simply no longer practicable, either as a normal or exceptional means of policy. On the other hand, the very existence of the terrifying threat of these weapons could be exploited politically in order either to maintain the existing state of affairs or to further the essential changes. When the nuclear level was reached, we moved from a war strategy to a strategy of potential threat; in other words, to a strategy of *deterrence*.

The consequences of the existence of this vast threat are considerable. It becomes so difficult to make the threat credible in the case of any stake not truly vital, that its stabilizing influence is effective only against the more traditional forms of warfare; these it prevents almost completely. As a result, peace is far more stable than before the advent of the nuclear weapon. But peace has no longer the absolute character it had in the last century: today it is possible to hurl insults at a nation, burn down its embassy, arrest its ships, send hired assassins into its country or give almost open support to political parties without war breaking out; formerly all this would have been unthinkable. Peace between contending nations has become 'war in peacetime' or cold war.

Furthermore, peace on the nuclear level is so stable that in spite of the existence of the nuclear weapon, we have in the last fifteen years seen a number of conventional wars of greater or lesser intensity and with a greater or lesser admixture of cold war and subversive practices (Korea, Indo-China, Laos, Suez, Sinai, Algeria, etc.); there have also been political confrontations such as Berlin and Cuba which would have been extremely serious in the past but which were settled by compromise.

Using cold war methods in sensitive areas and limited war in peripheral areas, a very wide field of action is open to indirect strategy. Because there now exists a nuclear level, warfare on the very large scale, whether nuclear or not, is tending to disappear, but as usual a compensating, though unexpected, factor has appeared – true peace is tending to disappear also.

In our world of today therefore we end with a four-tier (as opposed to a two-tier) strategy:

Peace – complete peace which hardly exists other than between allies and neutrals;

The level of war in peacetime or cold war – a form of non-military struggle between contending nations, the violence of which is increased by nuclear deterrence and ideological tensions;

The conventional level – the old form of armed contest, more exceptional and more limited than hitherto;

The nuclear level – a new and overriding factor in the international balance and a form of armed contest at once possible and morally inadmissible.

Certain of these 'type' levels may, moreover, be combined into composite procedures and these must also be examined:

The level of cold war including the very limited[1] use of conventional forces (Cuba, Laos, etc.);

[1] Termed by the Americans 'sublimited'.

The conventional level including the possible and more or less limited use of tactical nuclear weapons, a possible but hitherto untried form of armed conflict and one of the present methods of deterrence.

CLASSIFICATION AND GENERAL CHARACTERISTICS OF LEVELS OF USE OF FORCE

In any study of deterrence it is essential that the existence of these various levels be recognized. Each of the four levels represents a differing degree of the use of violence and is governed by special laws stemming from its political and psychological characteristics and from its technical factors. But before analysing them they must be correctly situated in relation to each other.

At first sight, one might be tempted to think that the four levels set out above are no more than subdivisions of the old levels, the old-style peace being divisible into peace and cold war, old-style war into conventional war and nuclear war. A broad-brush approximation of this nature has two disadvantages; it does not take account of the new, comparatively violent and horribly efficient character of cold war and it considers the nuclear level purely from the operational standpoint, failing to take account therefore of its very specialized qualities.

There is a second broad-brush classification: one might be tempted to regard peace as being solely the level of complete peace and therefore to think that the old level 'war' can now be divided into three: cold war, conventional war and nuclear war. This classification is just as mistaken. As we shall see in further detail in the next chapter, there is an essential difference between cold war and the conventional war and nuclear war levels; use of the conventional war and nuclear war levels is now more or less exceptional and when they are used, they have a definite beginning and ending, whereas the cold war level is in use continuously. One can try to deter conventional or nuclear war; one cannot deter cold war. Moreover, implicit in the cold war is the continuous use, either as a spur or a brake, of the threat of employment of the other levels: it is the existence of the other levels (particularly the nuclear level) which has led to intensification of the cold war beyond the limits hitherto set by custom and the prospects of success.

This seems to indicate a different arrangement of the various levels:

1 The level of *complete peace*; this is the level of the old-style peace in which the 'minor key' methods, inducement and persuasion, are employed in accordance with international peacetime usage.

2 The level of cold war, hitherto a somewhat exceptional situation but today a permanency. It is used in differing degrees of intensity and employs simultaneously violent action on a minor scale and the dissuasive or persuasive pressures of the conventional or nuclear threats. Thus the cold war profits from the existence of the whole spectrum of employment of force, but keeps the actual use of force within cold war limits; in other words it avoids the employment of conventional and nuclear weapons by continuous use of the strategy of deterrence. To repeat—it is at the level of the cold war that the full range of the strategy of deterrence is brought into play.

3 The levels involving the use of armed force:

(a) The level of conventional warfare; this implies essentially the use of conventional methods but combining them with cold war action and employing the dissuasive or persuasive pressure exerted by threats of extension of conventional warfare or recourse to nuclear warfare;

(b) The level of nuclear warfare; the essential feature here is the use of nuclear weapons combined with action on the conventional and cold war levels but at the same time making use of the dissuasive or persuasive pressure of the threat of further extension of nuclear warfare.

At each level, therefore,—except in the case of complete peace which does no more than mark the end of the scale—there will be a dialectic of action and deterrence, the action being the more restricted as the deterrence is more complete. At each of these levels there will be specific forms of action but their interaction upon the other levels (active or deterrent as the case may be) will invariably be clearly defined.

We must, therefore, seek to discover:

On the one hand the laws of deterrence applicable to the methods of action peculiar to each level;

On the other hand the laws of deterrence stemming from the inter-action between the various levels.

Finally, this classification of the four levels into three categories as we have been led to do above, has the advantage that it underlines the peculiar character of the cold war level; it is not peace but it does not involve the open and avowed use of military force. As we shall see, thanks to the nuclear deterrent, this level possesses poten-tialities of the greatest possible importance.

The problem with which we are about to deal, therefore, is that of the methods necessary to preserve true peace. The questions are: Is the nuclear weapon of itself adequate and equally is it indispen-sable? Are the other methods equally indispensable or are they merely useful? These are the cardinal questions posed by strategy in the nuclear age.

I shall pursue this quest in two stages.

In the first place we shall deal with the most simple bilateral prob-lem, that which has existed for some time between the United States and the USSR. Today this situation is theoretical but as we shall see, the problem itself is highly complex. We shall have to get down to the do-ray-me of this phenomenon in order to apply it sub-sequently to the real problem, multilateral deterrence.

This analysis will be found to be delicate at all times and some-times unrewarding. It leads however to conclusions which will clear the mind and therefore justify the effort made to reach them.

Two

Analysis of Bilateral Deterrence

In this chapter it will be assumed that two opponents only are confronting each other. The rest of the world does not exist. Against this background I propose to examine the reasons for and the lights and shades of deterrence at each level – and it will be seen that they differ considerably; I shall also deal with the relative degree of force from which this or that category of deterrence may be anticipated.

This analysis is basic to the remainder of the study. Unfortunately it is inevitably somewhat abstract.

Bilateral deterrence brings into play a series of actions and reactions which can be arranged in distinct families of concepts. In order to understand how it works, we must first analyse the conditions governing equilibrium or disequilibrium at each of the levels; in other words, we must examine the various deterrent situations and then analyse the changes in the balance of deterrence caused by the influence of the other levels. We shall then be in a position to seek to understand the principles governing the bilateral deterrent manœuvre, by which is meant a series of actions at the various levels synthesized with the object of producing maximum deterrence.

This is the plan I propose to follow.

1 ANALYSIS OF DETERRENCE SITUATIONS

ANALYSIS OF DETERRENCE AT THE NUCLEAR LEVEL

The nuclear weapon has forced us to take full account of the notion of deterrence; it has in fact promoted it to the status of a prime factor in strategy. The mechanics of deterrence at the nuclear level must therefore be dissected in detail. This is all the more necessary in that at the present time we are faced by nuclear theories sometimes contradictory and all too often based upon inadequate appreciation of the nature of the deterrence phenomenon – a highly complex affair as we shall see.

The nuclear risk

The basis of nuclear deterrence is the *certainty of the damage* which would result from use of these weapons, protection against them being no better than very incomplete.[1] The nuclear weapon therefore represents a 'destructive capability' so great that it cannot be disregarded nor can there be any doubt about the serious damage which it would inevitably produce. It is this *threat of destruction* which generates deterrence because of the undoubted level of *risk* implied.

The nuclear risk is so obvious that there is all too often a tendency merely to deal with it summarily and without analysing it. In fact only by analysing the nuclear risk can the scope and the nuances of nuclear deterrence really be understood.

In our systematic study of deterrence in the Institut Français d'Études Stratégiques we evaluated the risk as a percentage of a country's total resources liable to be destroyed by an enemy strike; we started by setting out a scale of risks in four typical categories and to these we allotted arbitrary figures as follows: risk nil, risk acceptable (0–2 per cent), risk justified by the stake (2–10 or 15 per cent), risk unacceptable except for a major stake (10 or 15–50 per cent), risk unacceptable whatever the stake (50–100 per cent).

But this initial attempt to classify and evaluate the risk does not fill the bill. In the first place, as we have just seen, the factor of the issue at stake has to be brought in, it being clear that deterrence is the result of an unfavourable comparison between the risk and the issue at stake. Mathematically deterrence should begin to operate when the risk becomes greater than the stake. Psychologically,

[1] See *Introduction to Strategy*, Chapter III, 'Nuclear Strategy'.

35

however, owing to the various factors of uncertainty, including the impossibility of arriving at a precise appreciation of the value of the stake, the risk exerts a deterrent effect well before it has reached parity with the stake. It should be added that comparison of the issues at stake for the two opponents indicates the level of tension of the conflict in which they are engaged.

The main qualification, however, attaching to any categorization of the nuclear risk lies in the essential distinction between the side which fires first and the side which must reply: he who fires first would appear to have all the advantages: he can choose his moment; he can make use of surprise; all his resources are intact. He who must reply, on the other hand, will have been taken by surprise and a proportion of his resources either destroyed or disorganized. There is therefore a noteworthy degree of dissymmetry between the attack and the riposte. Which should be taken as the yardstick for the nuclear risk?

For some time interest centred upon the attack: this was the period when people were primarily worried about the hypothesis of a surprise attack, a nuclear 'Pearl Harbour' and when they were drawn towards the preventive or pre-emptive attack.[1] Then people gradually began to realize that the likelihood of such an attack was becoming more remote as the riposte to it began to appear more certain and more destructive. Conversely, if the attack were highly effective, the riposte would be weak or problematical and in this case attack became increasingly probable. The conclusion was therefore reached that *capacity for riposte was the key to nuclear deterrence*, whereas *capability to reduce the riposte was the key to nuclear initiative*.

This simple concept is still a long way from being understood by everybody, as we shall see in a moment. In fact, if a first strike attack only becomes probable and therefore credible, because it is capable of achieving a significant reduction of the enemy's second strike riposte,[2] it becomes clear that its value lies basically in its ability to destroy the highest possible proportion of the forces the enemy will use for his riposte: the first strike must therefore pri-

[1] Preventive: the initiative entirely in the hands of the attacker. Pre-emptive: attack to forestall an enemy initiative thought to be imminent.
[2] First strike: action by that side which takes the initiative in the use of strategic nuclear weapons. Second strike: the enemy's nuclear riposte to the first strike.

marily be a counter-force strike,[1] otherwise it will merely invite a riposte still intact and therefore still too formidable. On the other hand, since deterring this attack depends upon fear of the riposte, the latter must be as invulnerable as possible to the first strike and its destructive capacity must be as formidable as possible from the point of view of the aggressor; it must therefore turn cities, factories and resources in general into hostages; *the second strike must accordingly be primarily a counter-value strike.*[2]

Bilateral nuclear situations

Proceeding on from these ideas, it should now be clear that our evaluation of the degree of nuclear stability stems directly from the *second strike dialectic*; in other words from a comparison between the effectiveness of the two sides' ripostes, effectiveness meaning the anticipated result from the use of their entire residual forces. It is therefore the relative level of effectiveness of riposte capability on the part of the two opponents which determines the 'nuclear situation'. By varying the relative situations of the two opponents and trying all possible combinations, one can arrive at a complete list of all imaginable bilateral nuclear situations. This analysis has been made in great detail in our basic study[3] to which the reader wishing for further particulars may refer. Here it is enough to point out the fact that there are four typical nuclear situations:

'*Absolute stability*' when both sides consider that they are threatened by a riposte which is unacceptable whatever the stake;

'*Absolute instability*' when each side is confident that there will be no riposte provided he fires first;

'*Absolute superiority*' to one side or the other (two situations), when one or the other is confident that if he fires first there will be no riposte (see Diagram 1, page 38).

Between these four absolute situations, and corresponding to intermediate levels of attack and riposte capability, there exist a number of compound situations; these form marginal zones, producing

[1] In other words, its target must be the enemy nuclear weapons.
[2] In other words, its targets must be primarily enemy resources and in particular his cities.
[3] In the Review *Stratégie*.

1. Bilateral deterrent situations at the nuclear level

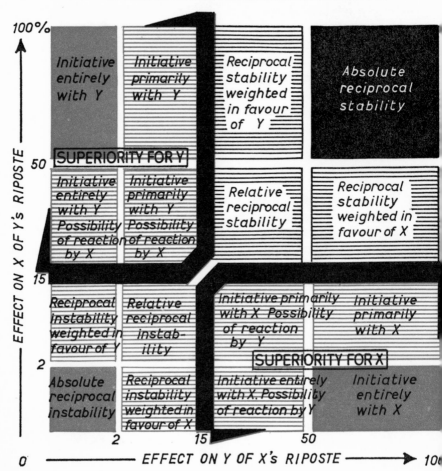

instability (if the risk of riposte in either direction is small),
superiority for one side or the other (if the risk of riposte in only
one direction is small), stability (if the risk of riposte is great but
acceptable in the case of a major stake).

This diagram is a good visual representation of this phenomenon;[1]
it brings out the striking point that the situations of instability, however they may arise, occur only if the risk of riposte is nil or very

[1] See the Review *Stratégie*.

38

small. As soon as the risk of riposte is no longer definitely small, we enter upon situations of more or less absolute stability. From this it is clear that the present situation as between the USSR and the United States is in the stable zone. Even as between Great Britain or France and the USSR it is not impossible to envisage the establishment of a sort of relative stability: the British or French capability merely has to be estimated at 10 or 15 per cent of Soviet resources.

The nuclear deterrence problem therefore in general falls within the sector comprising 'stability' situations.

Study of nuclear stability

This nuclear stability deserves careful analysis; qualities which it does not always possess are often ascribed to it, since people do not always differentiate between the various categories of stability.

It is true that if there are two opponents one of whom has, for instance, an effective riposte capability of 90 per cent (effective capacity to destroy 90 per cent of enemy resources) and the other an effective riposte capability of 15 per cent (effective capacity to destroy 15 per cent of enemy resources), they are in a situation of mutual deterrence—unless of course the stake is such that the stronger of the two is prepared to accept the idea of losing 15 per cent of his resources. This relative equilibrium between 15 and 90 has been taken as the basis of what is known as the 'equalizing power of the atom'. This phenomenon therefore implies a degree of equilibrium quite unthinkable with a similar ratio of conventional forces.

But 15 is a long way from being *equal* to 90. With a riposte capacity of 90 per cent of enemy resources, the stronger side has an absolute deterrent capability against the weaker side, whereas the latter has only a relative deterrent capability (limited to 15 per cent) against the stronger. The weaker side has only a *defensive deterrent* capability, valid merely for the protection of his own territory; the stronger side, on the other hand, can threaten to employ his 90 per cent capacity provided he is prepared to lose 15 per cent. The stronger can therefore exert an *offensive deterrent* effect, which the weaker side cannot; this deterrent effect may, for instance, enable the stronger side to prevent the weaker reacting to an attack against a third party or even against himself. In short, although direct and relative defensive deterrence is comparatively easy to achieve – the reason for the present high level of stability – indirect defensive deterrence is much more difficult because it presupposes an offensive deterrent capability and this in turn, in the last analysis, depends upon the ability to shoot first with the minimum of risk or at least to give the impression that one is prepared to shoot first. This is the vital problem of first strike credibility.

First strike credibility

Nuclear strategy is rather like one of those dreams when you are in a vast empty house opening one door after another from one room to another without ever reaching the end. We started from the nuclear risk, moved on to the first strike, thence to the importance of the riposte, thence to situations of equilibrium, and now we are back again faced with the necessity to preserve first strike credibility. One begins to wonder whether all this is not a luxury, a refinement, the preserve of very rich powers, and whether a defensive deterrent capacity is not enough.

This raises one of the most important, if not the most important, questions in nuclear strategy. In fact, however complicated the chain of argument, there is no denying the commonsense fact that the deterrent effect of the whole structure rests upon one very simple but vital thing, each side's fear of finding that the other fires first; for if no one fires first there will be no riposte, but if no one fears that someone else will fire first, there is no nuclear deterrence. The disappearance of nuclear deterrence would be a frightful catastrophe – in spite of the somewhat ill-considered view of certain well-known wiseacres – for we should then lose the benefit of the stability created by the atom in our rapidly evolving world. The problem of first strike credibility is therefore anything but a secondary problem. On the contrary, though many of our contemporaries do not realize it, it is the overriding security factor of our era. Three methods have been used or proposed concurrently in order to preserve a degree of credibility for the first strike.

The first method – and the only really satisfactory one – is to *make the first strike a rational act* by ensuring that one has the means of reducing the enemy's riposte to a level both morally and politically tolerable. To achieve this result means having either an adequate (in other words crushing) counter-force capacity or a highly efficient anti-aircraft and anti-missile interception system or both. The anticipated return from counter-force action has tended to shrink considerably, particularly since the development of Polaris submarines. As far as anti-missile interception is concerned, techniques are available but they raise problems of the most extreme complexity. It seems that the Americans have for the moment slowed down preparatory work on the anti-missile programme, preferring to devote their efforts to offensive methods. It is possible, on the other hand, that the Russians have achieved something in this field – at least they say so. It should be noted in this connection that anti-missile defence is at the moment the only antidote to the Polaris submarine threat, possibly the reason for the Soviet choice. It should also be noted that the anti-missile solution to the counter-force problem has a number of advantages:

(1) It is the best politically, since one does not have to take the responsibility of being the first to fire;

(2) It is applicable to the various categories of threat (ICBM, Polaris, aircraft);

(3) It may pay a very high dividend if the density of the enemy's first strike is not very great. On the other hand it is undoubtedly extremely complex; it is difficult to ensure that it keeps pace with attacking methods (which will undoubtedly include the use of decoys), and it can easily be saturated if the density level of the enemy first strike is high. At all events, the value of an anti-missile defence, though tactically defensive, is in fact strategically offensive since it safeguards riposte capability. Its possible development in years to come, perhaps by making use of stratospheric explosions, may considerably modify the present equilibrium. For the moment, however, it would seem that in spite of counter-force or anti-missile tactics, the weight of both the American and Soviet ripostes is enough to achieve a level of destruction far greater than anything which could justify the launching of a first strike.

The second method, seemingly unavoidable if the first method is not practicable, is to *ignore the irrationality* of launching the first strike and proclaim one's determination to make an automatic response in certain defined circumstances. Colour may be lent to the announcement of this decision by proclaiming publicly that authority to launch the strike has been delegated, thereby making it clear to the enemy that the strike will in fact be launched in the given circumstances. This method would at first sight seem to be highly effective. In fact, however, it comes up against the difficulty that an automatic launching of a first strike, the effect of which would be to evoke an annihilating riposte, would be tantamount to committing suicide. The credibility of a determination to commit suicide is not zero, but it is very small. If this method is to be adequately convincing, therefore, it must fulfil one of the following conditions: either suicide must be avoidable because the results of the first strike are sufficient considerably to reduce the enemy riposte (as in the first method), or alternatively he who has to take the decision must contrive to make his adversary believe that he is capable of acting in an irrational manner involving the destruction of his own people. The first supposition appears less and less possible as the strike forces become more invulnerable; the second can never be more than a last ditch solution in default of anything else calculated to keep the enemy in doubt, however small that doubt may be. In any event, this method is a form of declared threat which no one would wish to fulfil should the threat fail.

The third method consists of *rationalizing the irrational decision* to launch the first strike by eliminating any implication of challenge inevitably calling for response. A declaration is made that the first strike constitutes no more than a limited warning and that consequently there is no necessity for it to evoke a 'spasm' riposte. Moreover, to deter the enemy from making such a riposte, a large scale and invulnerable counter-city capacity is held in reserve. Under the umbrella of this deterrence, it is then stated that one is prepared to take limited or even 'sublimited' tactical or strategic nuclear action. The hope is that by this method some impression will be made on the enemy and that he will be persuaded to accept a compromise before any form of escalation has taken place. If this was not enough, the level of the argument would be raised and a counter-force attack launched, but still leaving the enemy population untouched in order to avoid forcing him into a counter-city riposte. If eventually there was no alternative to strategic counter-city action, this stage would only be initiated progressively by very limited partial attacks. The idea is that, faced with these increasing threats, one or other of the two participants would be the first to have had enough of this ghastly poker game and that the massive destruction of the paroxysmal nuclear exchange envisaged in 1955 would still have been avoided.

This method, Mr McNamara's latest (1964) doctrine, is more subtle than the second. It is nevertheless far from being ideal, for a number of serious criticisms can be made:

(1) The 'announcement' of a limited action relieves the enemy of the inhibitions which might stem from his fear of letting loose a catastrophe. By being humanized, war becomes conceivable and so less improbable.

(2) The use of warning strikes, if considered as a normal procedure and however firm the intention to keep them limited, carries with it the risk of initiating a chain reaction. This is highly dangerous.

(3) Acceptance of counter-city action, even on a limited scale, would appear to break all bounds of prudence and morality.

(4) The game being progressive and aiming at compromise, there is a risk that the enemy will not be prevented from laying hands in the early stages on valuable bargaining counters and so putting himself in an advantageous position for the ultimate negotiations.

(5) If escalation is to be avoided, this method must have at its disposal an invulnerable and highly formidable striking force; it cannot therefore be employed by second-rank nuclear powers.

(6) If the enemy has an efficient anti-missile defensive system, limited strikes, consisting of a few shots only, are more than likely to be intercepted.

These arguments are not without weight and it is regrettable that this method has been announced as *replacing* that of massive retaliation. A greater degree of deterrence and of flexibility would have been achieved if the two methods had been combined, leaving the enemy in doubt as to the type of reaction which he would provoke and preserving freedom of choice on the type of response best suited to the incident concerned.

But the most remarkable feature of this doctrine, now emerging as a factor of stability, is the appearance of a *concept of limited employment of nuclear weapons*. Under the influence of air strategy, which acted as midwife for nuclear strategy, the initial concept was dominated by the idea of destruction in its most violent possible form, termed the 'spasm'. The advantage offered by surprise and then by the first strike led people to construct a colossal rationalized machine for total destruction, with the object of preventing similar action by the enemy. But as it becomes obvious that this destruction can only be mutual, this concept loses its validity. Nuclear weapons then tend to fall into the same category as other weapons, which have never been used all-out other than exceptionally. Nuclear weapons tend to become what they should always have been: one of the factors in the overall game, the object of which is deterrence or the enemy's capitulation.

This concept may at the moment appear somewhat utopian since it is too closely related to the thinking of a bygone age. If, however, the problem is examined, the conclusion must be that in a situation of stability this is the only imaginable type of nuclear conflict – if indeed such a conflict is imaginable at all.

In any case it should be noted that neither the second nor the third methods above produce a satisfactory solution to the problem raised by the increasing stability of the nuclear level, and this stability runs the risk of giving the go-ahead to violent action at the other levels. We must be clear on this: if the establishment of a degree of nuclear stability is a grave danger – as I believe that it is – the only remedy is to find some method of re-establishing a certain nuclear instability.[1] Following this line of thought, there is only one real solution: to have available once more an adequate counter-force capability, achieved either by offensive action or by interception.

[1] The ultimate object is to obtain the maximum overall stability through deterrence.

The counter-value and counter-resources argument

This brings us back once more to an idea already touched on above; it now appears in a different light. Previously the object was to ensure that the first strike had a sufficient counter-force capability to reduce the enemy riposte to a tolerable level; this was a deterrent concept confined to the particular case then under consideration. At the point we have now reached, it appears that the question is one of preserving the validity of the entire nuclear deterrence system. It is therefore a problem of the first importance.

There are very divergent opinions on this subject. Numerous theorists on either side of the Atlantic–and apparently on either side of the Iron Curtain too–have come forward as protagonists of a theory of deterrence relying basically on the threat of destruction of major cities. They have recommended the formation of adequate limited and invulnerable retaliatory forces ('the finite deterrent') and in some cases have even found it desirable that the enemy should possess a comparable force. This idea is at the root of the majority of disarmament plans; indisputably it would result in a nuclear situation so stable that one wonders how nuclear deterrence could exert any influence upon the other levels. This strategy of equilibrium may be excellent for preventing nuclear war but, as we have seen, if our object is to avoid war as such, from the moment at which it achieves too complete a balance, it becomes a fallacy.

But these general arguments are reinforced by others of a technical nature. A considerable and doubtless increasing proportion of the retaliatory forces can now be made to all intents and purposes invulnerable by use of Polaris submarines, Minuteman in concrete silos and similar devices. Why then spend astronomical sums in building up a worthwhile counter-force capacity when in any case one is going to be subjected to an intolerable riposte? Some say that the Russians have been quite right not to embark upon a counter-force policy: with a comparatively small number of strategic weapons, they threaten the main American cities with destruction and that is quite enough to paralyse the far larger and far more costly American nuclear arsenal. Finally, is it really possible to differentiate between military targets (counter-force) and civilian

45

targets (counter-city)? Any attack on the former will inevitably entail considerable damage to the latter.

Is it possible to reach a conclusion on this theory? To solve this problem, we must go back to the basic ideas which I put forward in my *Introduction to Strategy*. We must at all costs avoid mistaking the secondary for the primary, and we must get the various ideas in logical order if we are to understand the essential characteristics of this phenomenon.

What is the problem? *The problems facing the Americans and the Russians are two different things.* The Americans are confronted by an enemy who, by tradition, carries on the offensive in the indirect strategy 'mode' using insidious methods; at the same time, in the direct strategy 'mode' he safeguards his own territory and acquisitions by powerful military forces. His total strategy is therefore offensive but as far as military strategy is concerned, he needs only a defensive capacity. It is against this background that the USSR has built up her striking force and it is against the same background that she accepted the compromise following the Cuba crisis. Looked at overall on the other hand, American indirect strategy is more of a defensive nature; it is, therefore, essential that they should have available a nuclear capacity with a certain offensive potential in order to persuade the Soviet Union not to overstep certain limits in their indirect infiltration process. It was to a large extent thanks to this offensive capability that the Americans were able effectively to call a halt in Cuba. It is therefore the fact that the total strategies of the two sides are of a different type which enables one to do without a counter-force capacity and forces the other at all costs to maintain such a capability at a level which cannot be disregarded. Finally it should be added that, although counter-force action must inevitably spill over to a serious extent onto the civil population, a counter-force capability differs radically from a counter-city capability: the former presupposes an ability to hit each of the force targets *separately*, whereas attack on the civil population necessitates merely generalized destruction, requiring far fewer projectiles (a rough minimum proportion is 1 to 14).[1]

---

[1] For instance, assuming that three projectiles each of one megaton would suffice to destroy an enemy launching site (and some specialists estimate that in the case of certain

But this initial diagnosis covers only a part of the problem. In fact in the existing state of affairs, it is essential to world peace that there should be at least *one* power capable of maintaining a deterrent potential at the nuclear level; it is also essential that this power, which as a result must preserve a certain offensive capability, should at the same time be a peaceable one. It is this which preserves the entire structure of deterrence.

To appreciate the importance of this fact, just imagine the position if another, not a peaceable, power was alone possessed of the same advantages: the situation would be intolerable. Then think of the position if the United States gave up their offensive deterrent capability, in other words, their counter-force capability: the result would be total neutralization of the nuclear level, making it possible both to embark on and then to extend vast conventional military conflicts provided they did not directly threaten the territory of the United States. This shows that the United States has been right to insist on maintaining a counter-force capability and that we all benefit thereby.

At this point a technical argument enters into the picture: counter-force capability is tending to become less and less effective not only because methods of protection are developing but also because, as nuclear forces increase in size, the laws of deterrence force us to retain the ability to destroy a larger and larger proportion of them in order to maintain an effective deterrent.[1] Moreover, with the present day counter-force technique (destruction of each weapon individually), the ratio required between the number of weapons to be fired and the number of weapons to be destroyed (see note on previous page) means that the two sides cannot engage in a

---

highly protected sites 18 to 24 projectiles each of 10 megatons would be necessary), to destroy 480 ICBM (60 per cent of the American ICBMs) it would be necessary to launch at a minimum 1,440 *rockets*; to destroy 60 per cent of the population of America, which is concentrated in 54 cities, would under normal conditions require only 108 *rockets*.

[1] Calculations show for instance that to reduce to less than 10 per cent an enemy counter-value capability of 50 per cent, our own counter-force capability must be 75 per cent (see Analysis by Institut Français d'Études Stratégiques in Review *Stratégie*).

counter-force capacity race.[1] Are we not therefore faced with an impossible situation? In other words, is not nuclear stabilization inevitable?

To understand this we must go back once more to the principles. The nuclear stabilization towards which we are moving is a phenomenon analogous to the stabilization of the fronts at the end of 1914. It stems from the fact that in the present phase of technical development, the tactical factors governing deterrence have reached a certain degree of preponderance. There was stabilization in 1914 because tactical mobility was small as compared to strategic mobility and because defensive capacity had largely outstripped offensive capacity. In the case of nuclear deterrence, mobility hardly appears to enter into it, but once more we are seeing defensive capacity being considerably increased at the expense of offensive capacity: the submarines and concrete silos of 1964 fulfil the same function as the trenches and barbed wire of 1915. This situation is neither inevitable nor permanent. Stabilization will remain complete only insofar as it proves impossible to reduce the influence of the tactical factor and recapture a certain offensive capacity. The efficiency of counter-force tactics must therefore be increased by the introduction of new techniques. This is where the effort should be made. It is perhaps what the Russians have done, if they have – as they claim – really developed an effective anti-missile weapon.

So the argument between the counter-force and counter-value theories resolves itself into a basic truth governing both: the starting point for strategy must not be that which is possible; we must discover what is necessary and try to achieve it. If that proves impossible, we shall at least have shown up the decisive factor and we ought not to be surprised if chance or the enemy finally succeed in fulfilling the necessary conditions. If it proves possible, we shall be the masters rather than the servants of evolution.

---

[1] Assuming that in order to destroy one enemy missile it is necessary to launch N nuclear weapons, each time one side puts one additional weapon into service, the other must put in N if he is to maintain his counter-force capability. Following the same rule, this first side would have to have N^2 weapons available in order to destroy N enemy missiles. For each side, therefore, the rule governing counter-force growth is a geometrical progression to the power of N^2.

Conclusions on bilateral nuclear deterrence

Setting aside the subtleties, the variable truths and all the controversies, the keystone of nuclear deterrence is counter-force capability because only that capability, provided it is adequate, can make the launching of the first strike credible and because it is the threat of launching the first strike which constitutes deterrence. Solutions based upon counter-value action cease to be credible as soon as the launching of the first strike will clearly evoke too devastating a response and whenever that sort of suicidal action is not justified by a vital (in the strict sense of the word) stake. This is the essence of bilateral nuclear deterrence. We shall see later that the laws of multilateral deterrence are somewhat different.

The fact that counter-force tactics are at present proving more and more difficult and their results becoming problematical in no way changes the conclusions above; but it does carry with it the corollary that the influence of nuclear deterrence is declining owing to a tendency towards stability which could eventually end in paralysis.[1] When we come to deal with the other levels we shall see what the repercussions of this may be.

It should be emphasized, however, that the present situation is of a transitory nature only and that it can at any moment be changed by some technical innovation, for instance those perhaps foreseeable in the field of missile interception.

This conclusion implies certain consequences which people all too often tend to overlook: in spite of the growing importance of the existence of nuclear weapons, but because of possible changes in the relationship between opposing destructive capabilities, the effectiveness of nuclear deterrence may change considerably, even in a situation of more or less absolute equilibrium, such as apparently exists between the two main opponents at the present time. At the nuclear level itself, there may be very varied situations: offensive deterrence if one side possesses a credible first strike; defensive deterrence if the equilibrium is so complete that it results in paralysis of all those forms of partial deterrence which rely upon the

---

[1] If nuclear deterrence lacked credibility minor conflicts could take place which one would have hoped to stop by a threat of escalation, however small.

risk implicit in the launching of a first strike above a certain level of violence or a certain magnitude of stake. As we shall see later, the influence of the nuclear level upon the other levels may at times be total, at times small and at times nominal.

The fact that nuclear deterrence is a variable quality means that it can be no permanent panacea, as people all too often try to make out; this means that the deterrence peculiar to the other levels may be so important that in certain cases it may prove overriding.

ANALYSIS OF DETERRENCE AT THE CONVENTIONAL LEVEL

The conventional level has been known for centuries. We are so familiar with it that we often overlook its essential features as with a member of our family. Moreover we have not been in the habit of considering it from the new angle of deterrence. I therefore propose to deal with this study using the method of analysis found necessary for nuclear deterrence. The reader will see that, as we dissect it, a number of unexpected aspects will emerge.

The conventional risk – victory by the enemy

In nuclear deterrence we started from the notion of the risk of immediate physical and calculable destruction. At the conventional level the risk which deters is less simple: it is the fear of being beaten, in other words of finding that victory has gone to the enemy. The difference between this and the nuclear level is considerable; nuclear destruction inevitably affects both sides in varying degrees but *conventional victory must go to one side only*. It is this which made conventional war fashionable down the ages: the expectation of success justified sacrifices because they would be rewarded by victory. As we saw above, this point of view should have changed with the advent of manufacturing age warfare, but the fact remains that the conventional level includes a sufficient element of uncertainty to account for the 'adventurism' with which people have so often gone into it. Moreover expectation of success has often been bilateral. Because of this expectation of success the risk entailed by war was accepted complacently. Deterrence was non-existent or very small and this applied to both sides.

In the light of this particular aspect of the conventional level I have been led to take as the basis of analysis of conventional deterrence the *dialectic of expectation of victory* on the part of the two opponents. I have divided the level of expectation into four categories on a descending scale as for nuclear deterrence and I have tried to set out a complete series of bilateral situations stemming from all the possible combinations of varying intensity of 'expectation of victory' on the part of the two opponents.

Bilateral conventional situations

This dialectic of the expectation of success is laid out graphically in diagram No. 2 (page 52).

Naturally there will be found here the same absolute bilateral situations as in the diagram for the nuclear level (reciprocal stability, reciprocal instability, superiority for one or other of the opponents); equally there are the same intermediate fringe situations of relative stability, instability or superiority. The point which leaps to the eye, however, is that where, in the nuclear diagram, there were stable situations, in the conventional diagram there is a zone of unstable situations. In other words *the conventional level tends to become unstable as soon as expectation of victory is anything but infinitesimal.* This is of course a purely theoretical statement and it should be considerably tempered in the light of the psychological factors such as inhibition and uncertainty; in fact the zone of conventional instability can be considerably reduced but the fact remains that the conventional level is basically an unstable level just as the nuclear level tends towards stability.

Balancing off the nuclear level exactly, therefore, deterrence at the conventional level in general presents itself as a problem within the sector comprising situations of instability.

Study of conventional instability

If the 'expectation of success' creates instability, what sort of instability is it exactly? There can be no question here of recapitulating the whole strategic problem of traditional military victory and

2. Bilateral deterrent situations at the conventional level

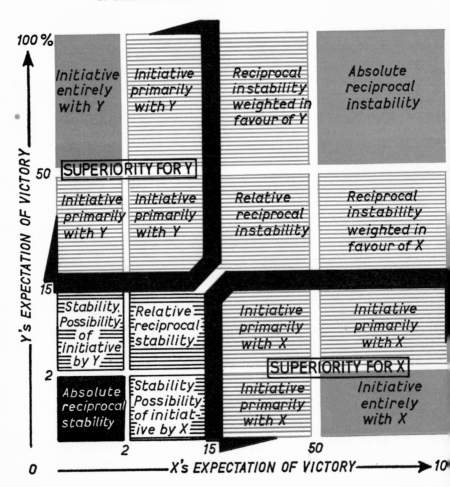

moreover our study must be confined to its true subject, deterrence, not war. It must be realized that conventional deterrence is not the result of a 'victory capability' analogous to 'destructive capability' at the nuclear level; that would be a material factor calculable in figures; in fact it is a function of the *opinion* formed of the enemy's ability to achieve victory.

But in conventional war forecasts of the results of a conflict stem directly from the theoretical concepts worked out and accepted by military leaders. Each side will estimate the potentialities of the other side in the light of his own doctrine: in 1939, for instance, the Maginot Line did not deter Germany whose doctrine was offensive but the Siegfried Line did deter France because France was a believer in fortifications. *The game of conventional deterrence must therefore be played with the enemy's doctrines as a yardstick.*

On the other hand in the conventional field there is a dialectic between the offensive and the defensive comparable to that between counter-force and counter-value tactics in the nuclear field. Nevertheless here again the differences are considerable. The conventional defensive, if successful, prevents an enemy victory: its deterrent effect is limitative; its counterpart, counter-value tactics, which as we have seen are basically defensive and deterrent, would result, if successful, in the complete destruction of the enemy. The conventional offensive aims at military victory and conquest of the enemy's territory, whereas counter-force tactics, which are essentially offensive, aim to limit the extent of the devastation. Thus each of the comparable components at the conventional and nuclear levels has similar characteristics but their symbols (plus or minus) are reversed – a good illustration of the contrast between these two levels.

For this reason therefore, whereas the problem of nuclear deterrence consists primarily in the search for instability, that of conventional deterrence is one of reinforcing stability.

How to reinforce conventional stability

This was the line of reasoning instinctively followed between the two world wars when people were trying to preserve the peace. The solutions adopted at this period showed how little the phenomenon of deterrence was understood.

We tried by an equipment and mobilization effort, supported by coalitions and military alliances, to bar Germany's way with conventional forces of the greatest possible size, reinforcing their defensive potential by fire power and fortifications.

The error made was twofold. On the one hand, as we have already seen above, we tried to deter, basing ourselves upon our own defensive doctrines, not upon those of the enemy. But on the other hand, and even more important, we committed the error of believing that it was possible to deter by making the enemy's victory more difficult; in fact in order to deter at the conventional level, he should have been made to fear victory by us. Hitler could only have been stopped pursuing his plans by a powerful offensive capacity such as could have been achieved by armoured forces (vainly advocated by the best minds of the time) supported by an efficient air force.

So, contrary to our own doctrines and the views of the pacifists, it was by offensive not defensive capacity that we should have been able to deter, just as at the nuclear level true deterrence is achieved through a counter-force capacity.

But contrary to what happens at the nuclear level, we could not by this method have achieved true stability at the conventional level: as each side developed its offensive capacity, the situation would have become increasingly unstable; each side would have seen a great military prospect opening up before it and would have been increasingly tempted by the spirit of adventure; the slightest incident would have been enough to let loose the cataclysm, as happened in 1914.

We have uncovered here a vital aspect of deterrence which, paradoxical though it may seem, is nothing less than a law: *a conventional armaments race produces instability, whereas a nuclear armaments race produces stability*; the reason is that the one conjures up pictures of possible victory, whereas the other increases the certainty of mutual destruction.

This highly important conclusion is supported both by the stability of recent years and by the instability which gave rise to the great twentieth-century military conflicts; it shows how great would be the danger should nuclear deterrence disappear as a result, for instance, of an ill-judged disarmament agreement. The conventional level is unstable by nature and with modern armaments war at this level can be most devastating.

In fact, as we shall see later, only one really effective method has so far been found of stabilizing the conventional level – *the introduction of nuclear weapons into the conventional level*. This has two advantages: by the threat of employment of a new weapon untried in battle complete uncertainty is created as to the tactical results of a battle and therefore as to the entire course of a campaign; secondly, by the employment of low-yield nuclear weapons fear is created of the possibility of escalation on to the strategic nuclear level; the stability achieved at the nuclear level is therefore extended to the conventional level. Here again the logical conclusions appear to be the exact opposite of many currently held opinions based on instinct rather than reasoning.

Conclusions on deterrence at the conventional level

In the foregoing rapid analysis I have designedly systematized the successive conclusions as far as possible, at the risk at times of some-what distorting the truth which is invariably more complex than the explanations I have put forward. The reason is that when dealing with the subject of conventional deterrence, I wished to bring out its most typical aspects in order to highlight the contrast between conventional deterrence and nuclear deterrence and also the laws peculiar to deterrence at the conventional level which we know so well but understand so little. Even, however, taking account of all the necessary lights and shades, the conclusion remains that the conventional level is by nature unstable and that it is just as difficult to achieve stability here as it is to achieve instability at the nuclear level.

But the fact that these two levels with diametrically opposed characteristics exist side by side can be utilized to make good the major disadvantages of each: by linking the two levels, the nuclear and the conventional, primarily by means of tactical nuclear weapons, the conventional level can be given the stability it lacks and the basic risk of instability can be restored to the nuclear level; this it must have if it is to continue to play its role as the great stabilizer.

Study of the possibilities of deterrence at the cold war level is a new idea. It comes as a natural extension of the line of thought imposed on us by the nuclear weapon but *a priori* there is nothing to show that it is feasible.

In fact the further away one gets from the more violent forms of conflict, the hazier does the notion of the risk become. Yet it is the risk which is the instrument of deterrence.

Analysis of the risk in cold war

What type of risk is there liable to be in cold war? At first sight this question would appear difficult to answer, if only because cold war actions may take so many different forms; what, for instance, is there in common between support of a revolution, a trade treaty or diplomatic pressure? Nevertheless if we do not let ourselves be discouraged by the complexity of the problem and if we therefore continue to search for an overall explanation, it will be seen that, compared to the other levels, the cold war level has one fundamentally distinctive characteristic: *there is no question of preventing cold war; it has already been in progress for a long time* and it shows itself here and there in barely perceptible ways. Its minor manifestations, moreover, are so insidious that its outbreak is often impossible to detect. The cold war level is more than merely unstable; it is in a state of constant flux.

This initial conclusion opens up a whole vista of consequences in logic: the object of deterrence at the other levels is to bar the use of force by the enemy, in other words to prevent him reacting in a manner which would constitute the formal opening of a certain defined type of hostility; at the cold war level deterrence can only aim to prevent the development of the crises and latent tensions inherent in a permanent struggle between two opposing powers. The place of preventive action is taken by prophylactic action. This is therefore no truly deterrent procedure but is in fact a *strategy of action*. With strategy as a starting point the whole thing becomes clear: at the cold war level the problem is to bring this 'minor key' form of warfare to a victorious conclusion. To do this we must follow the well-known great principles governing any form of conflict; I dealt with them in my *Introduction to Strategy*:[1] we have to deprive the enemy of his freedom of action while at the same time preserving our own, so as to be able to achieve the objective we have set ourselves. The key to the whole thing is freedom of action and *in cold war the risk is simply that of the loss of freedom of action.*

Freedom of action in cold war

Now at last we have got the criterion we have been looking for. It merely remains, if possible, to draw the correct conclusions from it. What is the essential feature of freedom of action in cold war? In this form of warfare, in which force is invariably disguised and insidious, everything below a certain degree of violence is in fact possible because it cannot in practice be prevented. Looked at from this angle, within the narrow limits of cold war, true freedom of action should be total. We know only too well, however, that this is not the case, and that a whole range of differing considerations come into play tending to paralyse initiative. This means that freedom of action is in general limited not so much by physical dispositions as by the psychological climate and more specifically by the *psychological climate of international opinion.* This is the governing factor in deterrence at the cold war level.

When dealing with indirect strategy[2] I brought out the fact that this type of conflict is won primarily by means of a manœuvre conducted on the world chessboard 'to paralyse the enemy by a multitude of deterrent checks somewhat as the Lilliputians tied up Gulliver'; I called this psychological manœuvre, carried out by political, diplomatic, economic and military means, the 'exterior manœuvre'.

Once the victim is thus isolated and mesmerized, the interior manœuvre is merely a matter of execution. There are of course cases in which the 'animistic cohesion' (in Ludendorff's phrase) of the

---

[1] See *Introduction to Strategy*, Chapter IV, 'Indirect Strategy'.
[2] Ibid.

3. Bilateral deterrent situations at the cold war level

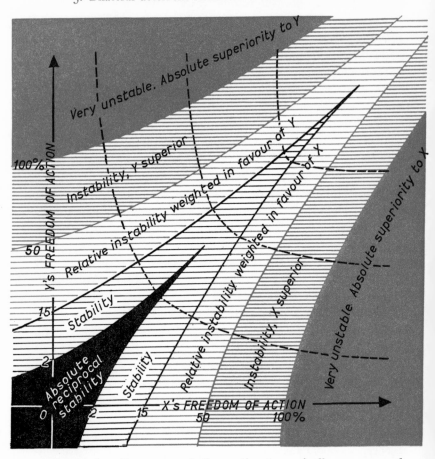

The broken line curves indicate diagrammatically an assumed constant product of the interplay between the opposing freedoms of action at a given level of intensity of conflict. Each curve represents a different level of intensity.

victim is such that there is no foothold for direct cold war action (Berlin and Israel for instance), but one wonders whether this cohesion would stand up for any length of time to an unfavourable international climate. In any case it is still the international chessboard which is in most cases decisive and it is by action there that the best level of deterrence can be achieved.

Bilateral cold war situations

The question now is whether it is possible to work out various bilateral cold war situations as we have done for the other levels and whether they can be shown graphically; the diagram would have to deal this time not with the dialectic of opposing destructive capacities nor with that of the expectation of victory but with the dialectic of freedom of action.

Bilateral cold war situations are clearly the same as those of the other levels: superiority, inferiority, equilibrium, instability with all the shades of emphasis from the absolute to the relative; the meaning of these terms, however, will be different since we are dealing with a struggle, not with the problem of preventing the initiation of a conflict. At the other levels both sides might be subject to considerable temptation to initiate the conflict, producing a situation of absolute reciprocal instability; at the cold war level, however, this cannot be, since everything depends on freedom of action. Looked at from the point of view of a struggle between two opponents, this freedom of action is the subject of a dialectic confrontation. From this point of view *the freedom of action of one of the opponents will invariably circumscribe that of the other.*

If an attempt is now made to set out this concept in diagrammatic outline and taking as the axes the freedom of action of the two opponents as in Diagram No. 3 (page 58), the curves plotting the various situations will be found to produce a picture in which the opposing freedoms of action are constant. This representation has the advantage of bringing out three important points:

(1) There are no reciprocal unstable situations as with the other levels;

(2) Situations of absolute reciprocal stability only exist when the freedom of action of both sides is very small, in other words when both sides are totally impotent;

(3) Situations of relative equilibrium (reciprocal stability) when freedom of action on each side is equal, are highly precarious and can turn rapidly into situations of absolute superiority for one side or the other.

For those who are not convinced by this mathematical type of explanation it should be added that this diagram brings out a characteristic feature of the cold war: any equilibrium is highly precarious and as soon as it is disturbed, a snowball phenomenon occurs which may well turn into a completely uncontrollable avalanche. Action is therefore required in situations of relative equilibrium, in other words when the first symptoms appear, otherwise it will be too late. This shows that at the cold war level possession of the initiative and offensive action are of overriding importance but carry with them the risk of letting loose phenomena out of all proportion to the immediate object in view; examples are Russian Communism, the seed of which was sown by Germany in 1917, Lawrence's Arabism, American anti-colonialism, etc.

Conclusions on deterrence at the cold war level

This study of deterrence at the cold war level brings out clearly its basic characteristics; its complexity is such that it merits the close analysis we have had to make of it.

(1) The cold war level is one of continuously shifting struggle. Total deterrence in the nuclear sense of the word does not apply here. The cold war equivalent is a strategy aiming at freedom of action.

(2) Freedom of action depends to a great extent upon the international climate and therefore upon the effect of the exterior manœuvre which will take place outside the area where it is intended to take action.

(3) Cold war equilibrium is particularly unstable and calls for initiative and offensive action at the risk of letting loose possibly uncontrollable phenomena.

Finally it should be noted that this study of the cold war level has brought out the fact that this level is one of continuous action; deterrence here is of a type entirely different from that at the other levels, where use of conventional or nuclear weapons is involved: at these latter levels deterrence is based on a number of bilateral situations, decided to a large extent by the ratio of the forces involved; these situations are so constricting that they may end in complete paralysis at these levels, all the more so since armed action is necessarily always limited in time, even when it is not barred for considerable periods. At the cold war level, on the other hand, deterrence is always relative and partial, all the more so since action at this level is, in one form or another, continuous. The laws of the cold war level therefore – and in particular the diagram illustrating the instability of the various situations – are in fact laws of action in general, in other words laws of strategy.

When therefore deterrence has contrived to bar the use of conventional or nuclear weapons, the cold war level emerges as the level of total strategy.

This confirms, if confirmation was necessary, that the cold war level is *the* modern operational level *par excellence*. It is the favourite field for indirect strategy since the immediate material risks involved are practically zero; but it demands the greatest vigilance, for the phenomena to which it gives rise are frequently greater than had either been foreseen or can be controlled by those involved. The economy of blood and effort achieved thereby is frequently out-weighed by cataclysms more serious than those which the participants were congratulating themselves at having avoided.

Its basic instability and the unforeseeable nature of its consequences makes the cold war a happy hunting ground for would-be political wizards.

This is yet another reason for trying to discover some subtle method of stabilizing this level eventually. It is a highly delicate subject which I have only touched on here; it must be the subject of a later study.

2 INTERACTION BETWEEN THE DIFFERENT LEVELS

As we have just seen, each of the levels has its own characteristics and its own particular laws. It now remains to see what influence they can exert upon each other, whether they spread a stabilizing influence or alternatively disseminate and magnify disequilibrium. I shall deal with these two phenomena in this order: first deterrence, second escalation.

DETERRENT INTERACTION

Influence of the nuclear level

Theoretically, as we have seen, the degree of nuclear deterrence may differ considerably depending upon the nature of the equilibrium produced by the nuclear forces. According to the degree of deterrence achieved, the influence of the nuclear level upon the others may be total, partial or non-existent. In the latter two cases, deterrence at the other levels must rely upon the methods pertaining to those levels. This being so, we have already concluded that conventional forces are both important and necessary, their role being either to round off nuclear deterrence if it is not complete, or even to replace it if its influence on the conventional level is negligible. The recent pronounced tendency on the part of the United States towards substantial reinforcement of conventional forces in Europe is, therefore, evidence of a pessimistic appreciation of the nuclear weapon's influence upon the conventional level.

It is of some interest to look at the present situation in detail. If the deterrent effect of the nuclear level is to extend to the other levels, this presupposes in the first place that the actions at these other levels which it is desired to deter are of a nature sufficient to justify launching the first strike. But as we have seen, the credibility of the launching of a first strike at the nuclear level is in general low. In other words, the deterrent effect of the nuclear level upon the other levels will be effective only if nuclear action involves no more than acceptable (in other words, minor) risk, meaning that the nuclear situation is unstable with a clear superiority to the side which wishes to deter. As we have seen, this situation is exceptional and it is for this reason that such intensive efforts have been made to give to nuclear action a minimum of credibility in spite of the stability of the situation. The conclusion, therefore, is that, except in particularly favourable circumstances, the deterrent effect produced upon the other levels by the threat of nuclear action is at a low level of credibility and its deterrent value almost negligible.

Nevertheless, the mere existence of the nuclear level with its inherent dangers produces another sort of deterrence, less definite but more effective: even if there is no fear that some action undertaken (at the conventional level, for instance) might be enough to cause the other side to launch the first strike, there may well be fear lest the more or less unforeseeable sequels to this action might lead to escalation to the nuclear level. Instead of the direct and automatic stabilization resulting from clear nuclear superiority to one side, the existence of the nuclear level creates an atmosphere of caution, essentially a stabilizing factor. This caution means that in general people will not initiate action on too large a scale. As against this, action on a minor scale, if necessary repeated, will not be subject to deterrence—a procedure particularly applicable to the cold war level.

To sum up, in general the nuclear level exerts a powerful stabilizing influence, but this influence can really only extend to the conventional level and then only in the case of action on a relatively large scale.

It is for this reason, as was emphasized when dealing with the conventional level, that it is essential for the conventional and nuclear levels to be firmly linked by the threat of employment of tactical nuclear weapons. Only by paying this price—and accepting the risk—can nuclear deterrence be made fully effective at the conventional level.

As far as the cold war level is concerned, in general it is not subject to the influence of nuclear deterrence.

Influence of the conventional level

Can the conventional level exert a deterrent influence upon the neighbouring levels?

The conventional level can exert an influence upon the cold war level; it will do so as soon as there is fear lest cold war action lead to military intervention capable of reversing the position: the Hungarian revolt in 1956 showed up one of the limitations to freedom of action in cold war; the capacity to intervene and dominate by force is a most powerful deterrent threat.[1] This is the justification for the maintenance of highly mobile and adequately powerful reserves.

The nuclear level being already stable on its own, one may well wonder whether the conventional level has any part to play here. Historically it did exert an influence during the early 1950s when the USSR had no striking force and was faced by the emergent nuclear force of the United States. It is difficult today to evaluate the deterrent effect of Soviet dispositions at that period, but it is fair to say that they may well have had a certain measure of effect in view of the force ratio of the time: the very great strength of the USSR in conventional forces was a military objective out of all proportion to the destructive capacity then possessed by the United States. The USSR developed their defensive tactics logically, protecting themselves effectively against nuclear explosions by a policy of going underground; a considerable proportion of the Soviet forces might therefore have survived; merely by their survival they would have represented a formidable offensive potential for the subsequent conquest of Europe, and Europe was at the time defenceless. This instance shows that in particular circumstances conventional forces can exert a noticeable deterrent influence upon the nuclear level. However, now that the destructive capacity of nuclear weapons has reached its present day level, the deterrent effect exerted upon the nuclear level by conventional forces is a much more problematical matter.

Nevertheless it should be emphasized that the present day tendency towards limited employment of tactical and strategic nuclear weapons might, if confirmed, give once more to conventional forces a certain power of deterrence over the strategic nuclear level. We might in fact find ourselves back in a situation analogous to that of the USSR in 1950, when the probability of survival of some conventional forces played a deterrent role *vis-à-vis* the launching of nuclear war.

---

[1] It should be noted nevertheless that if on this occasion we had given even indirect support to the Hungarians, Soviet intervention might have been a failure.

Influence of the cold war level

The cold war level, being the most restrained and the most insidious, would not at first sight appear to constitute a sufficient threat to prevent armed intervention at a higher level, if the factors operative at that level fail to deter. Yet here the historical example of the 1950's shows that the phenomena of deterrence are sometimes more effective on the psychological than on the material plane. When, after 1945, the USSR undertook her great Peace Congress campaign to arouse world conscience against the use of the nuclear weapons she did not possess, she evoked a considerable response from the majority of countries. No one can say whether this campaign could have prevented anything, since no one was at the time wishing to start a war; nevertheless it did indisputably create an atmosphere of opposition to the use of nuclear weapons and it gave rise to important inhibitions, which no doubt played some role; instances are Korea at the time of the MacArthur incident and Indo-China in connection with plans for intervention at Dien-Bien-Phu. This psychological inhibition is a factor which makes it very difficult to use nuclear weapons against a non-nuclear nation.

The deterrent influence of the cold war level upon the conventional level may equally prove decisive. Here we have the unhappy example of the Suez operation in 1956; despite certain (in fact negligible) nuclear aspects, this operation was brought to a halt at the moment of success by cold war action. A similar situation arose in the case of the protection of the FLN 'sanctuaries' in Tunisia and Morocco and also in that of the expulsion of the Soviet Union from bases in Albania.[1] The moral impossibility of carrying out certain military actions constitutes a deterrent at least as powerful as all material threats.

This, in a word, is the importance of the cold war level.

THE DANGER OF ESCALATION

Over each of these levels, stable or unstable, lowers the great threat

[1] In 1961 there was growing tension between the Kremlin and Tirana, a pro-Soviet *coup d'état* took place in Albania in February/March but failed. The Soviet Union was in no position to impose its will upon the Albanian leaders and in May was reduced to removing its submarines from the Valona base.

of the ascent to the nuclear paroxysm, which has come to be known as 'escalation'.

Much use has been made of this possibility to support the most varied theories for or against the nuclear weapon, whether strategical or tactical. The inevitability of escalation is the bogey of the nuclear disarmers and public opinion. The same threat of escalation is the essential argument of the protagonists of nuclear deterrence. In general, ideas on escalation remain highly subjective and vague; they must not be allowed to develop into an irrational or fatalist creed.

There are two possible types of escalation: spontaneous escalation resulting from action on the spot, and escalation resulting from decisions taken at the responsible level.

Spontaneous escalation

Spontaneous escalation by action on the spot makes a good story: an airman goes mad and sets fire to the world, a general loses his head and gives the fatal order, etc. Obviously neither airmen nor generals are proof against aberrations and weaknesses, but this type of accident could only produce a catastrophic effect if at the same time there existed a risk of escalation by responsible decision, a problem which we will look at in a moment. Since, however, it is obviously wise to reduce the probability of such accidents to the minimum, very extensive security measures have been taken and are continually being reinforced: weapons are permanently and closely guarded by special units with numerous personnel constantly on the watch for alert orders; launching orders must arrive by two different channels, crosschecking each other; finally, the safety catches on the weapons themselves can only be released by coded electronic messages. Precautions are so strict that one is inclined to fear that the riposte, if ordered, might be delayed. In spite of all these safeguards, one cannot be sure that an accident cannot happen. All that can be said is that it is in any case highly improbable and that the 'hot line' may well make it even more so.

Voluntary planned escalation

There remains the danger of voluntary escalation brought about by the development of the conflict. Here again a distinction must be drawn between escalation resulting from measures prepared in advance and that produced by decisions taken under the pressure of events.

Measures prepared in advance may prove very dangerous because their quality of automaticity may evoke irrevocable reactions: this was the position in the nuclear field during the 'massive retaliation' period, when a serious, but not necessarily vital, incident could have provoked a decision to riposte in a moment of aberration caused, for instance, by false information; at the present moment the fact that standing orders to use nuclear weapons are given to unit commanders (submarine commanders, for instance) should nuclear attack put them out of radio communication, might give rise to unfortunate decisions during a period of tension, when some electronic disturbance might be thought to be caused by nuclear explosions. It should be noted at once, however, that such hypothetical situations have become totally unreal ever since the spectre of the immediate strategic riposte has been removed from nuclear tactics thanks to the existence of a powerful and invulnerable retaliatory force. The time is now past when one side might feel forced to launch its rockets before they were destroyed, in other words as soon as the launching of the enemy salvo had been detected – possibly on false information. Now, thanks to the Polaris submarine and Minuteman in hardened emplacements, time is available to await confirmation of the attack before taking the decision to riposte. Retaliation – which will be counter-city – can afford to wait a while: it will be none the less formidable for that.

This recent stabilization of the strategic riposte (due to Kennedy's action) does not eliminate the risk of escalation by automatic reaction, since comparable stabilization has not been achieved in the tactical field:

(1) Anti-aircraft defence employs ground-to-air rockets with nuclear warheads; they would inevitably be used against massed bomber attacks and this might lead to confusion resulting in a nuclear riposte.

(2) Land forces possess tactical nuclear weapons, the use of which

is subject to Presidential decision. We shall be dealing with the problem of this decision later, but it should be noted here that if the land forces are being overrun, it will be difficult to refuse military commanders use of their tactical nuclear weapons. 'Tactical' escalation is therefore very probable as soon as aggression reaches a certain level of gravity.

As was noted in passing when dealing with the various levels, this possibility has the considerable advantage that it maintains a high degree of deterrence at the conventional level, which would otherwise be in danger of being very unstable. As with everything to do with deterrence, the result therefore is security achieved through danger.

Progressive voluntary escalation

But this danger remains limited only to the extent that it is incapable of evoking a strategic riposte. The whole problem of escalation therefore comes down to the question whether the use of a few tactical weapons, either by accident or to avert a local defeat, may possibly, or must necessarily, let loose the great mutual holocaust.

The real great danger therefore is that the leaders – not the military leaders but the political leaders at the highest level – may be carried along by events. We must therefore see how the problem will look to them.

Objectively, at each threshold escalation is the result of a decision the object of which is to avoid something worse: you fire first in order to prevent the other man killing you. If this decision be analysed, it will be seen that there are a certain number of factors, some leading to restraint – and so to stability, others to action – and so to escalation.

As we have already seen, the problem looks very different depending upon whether it is a case of a tactical or a strategic riposte.

In the tactical field, the decision to use nuclear weapons depends upon two types of consideration working in opposite directions: the desire to defeat an enemy attack and the fear of embarking on a process which may lead to mutual suicide. The latter consideration is obviously overriding. For this reason everything in fact depends upon the stability of the strategic level.

In the strategic field, we are faced with the same dilemma considerably intensified: are we to initiate nuclear action which would reduce the enemy's potential or force him into a compromise by demonstrating to him our determination to resist; alternatively, are we to do nothing from fear that there may be a reaction out of all proportion to the issue at stake? The key to the logical solution of this dilemma lies in analysis of the nuclear situation.

From the material point of view, the existence of a powerful and effective counter-force capability is a factor in favour of escalation: the side which possesses it is tempted to fire first in order to reduce to an acceptable level the danger of an enemy riposte; the side threatened by it is tempted to fire first in order to make use of his full destructive capacity before it is considerably reduced. Each side is therefore tempted to undertake preventive action. It is for this reason that counter-force capability has a de-stabilizing effect. As opposed to this, any more or less invulnerable counter-city destructive capability exerts a stabilizing influence: he who possesses it is certain at all times of being able to produce a devastating riposte, whereas for him who is threatened by it, there is no further object in firing first; if, however, counter-city destructive capability is not invulnerable, the side possessing it cannot afford to wait for the first enemy strike and will therefore be tempted to reply to non-nuclear aggression by nuclear escalation.

From the psychological point of view, it has been shown that uncertainty concerning the relationship between the respective nuclear forces is a stabilizing factor, whereas uncertainty regarding the enemy's determination may play a dangerous role, since it may lead to the acceptance of wrongly estimated risks. Fear may accelerate the decision to act by whichever side is materially better able to face escalation; fear may, on the other hand, play a stabilizing role if the material situation appears unfavourable for escalation.

We can therefore now draw up a table comparing the favourable and unfavourable factors:

Escalation	Stabilization
1 Large counter-force capacity on our side; enemy counter-city capacity vulnerable + fear	Enemy counter-city capacity invulnerable + fear
2 Own counter-city capacity vulnerable	Own counter-city capacity invulnerable
3 Determination	Doubt
4 Mistaken appreciation of the enemy determination	Uncertainty regarding relationship of respective forces
5 Unacceptably serious conventional defeat	Conventional equilibrium

Conclusions

This diagrammatic balance sheet shows that in the present situation, when the retaliatory forces are partially invulnerable, the balance of *probability* is in favour of stability. At this time, therefore, it may be anticipated that limited employment of nuclear weapons would not lead to escalation; this is a reason both for satisfaction and anxiety, since the threat of escalation plays a stabilizing role and its absence may make possible serious collisions at the cold war and even at the conventional level, thereby producing fresh risks of escalation. Fortunately there is no certainty that this stability will continue.

In a situation of nuclear stability, the conventional and cold war levels are of considerable importance since from them stem the errors leading to escalation.

These are as follows:

(1) A political or strategic stake of too great importance from the enemy point of view (e.g. Cuba);

(2) An over-important conventional military success;

(3) An error in estimating the enemy's determination (e.g. Cuba).

These three potential errors in total strategy show how essential it is that the game should at all times be played with delicacy and restraint. Escalation does not result from some sort of automatic mechanical process but it may be produced by the combined effect of two overlapping errors in manœuvre: an over-bold action countered by too elemental a response. Escalation is therefore not impossible. The experience of the Cuba crisis however, when each side gave proof of a high level of caution and realism, justifies the conclusion that *escalation is becoming less and less likely*.

3 THE BILATERAL DETERRENT MANŒUVRE

A deterrent manœuvre is a delicate game combining the threat of danger and caution on the part of the players. Neither of the two sides wishes to go to the limit since that would lead to his own demise but each is trying to prove by some visible action that he has greater determination than his opponent and that this determination is justified by certain trumps in his hand, which he has managed to keep secret. It is a ghastly poker game in which both players have sweaty hands, a lump in their throat and a racing pulse.

The example of Cuba

The Cuba crisis showed the sort of thing this manœuvre might be, at any rate at the more restricted levels of violence.

From 15 July 1962 the Russians proceeded to install in Cuba modern equipment which they pretended was solely defensive. On 4 and 13 September President Kennedy *declared* that if this armament was not in fact defensive, 'most serious questions would be raised'. He ordered aerial photography and *asked Congress* to authorize mobilization of 150,000 reservists. This potential threat, however, was not enough to stop the Russians, for on 15 October photographs finally proved that IRBM were being installed in Cuba. At the same time (the very next day) Malinovsky *declared* that Soviet rockets would be launched 'at the first alert signal'. The Americans therefore had to step up the threat.

On 22 October Kennedy *announced* that Cuba was in 'quarantine' and the OAS *voted* a resolution authorizing the United States to use force. Cuba mobilized. On 25 October, Kennedy sent a written *message* to Kruschev demanding dismantlement of the military bases in Cuba, failing which he would take fresh measures. At the same time it was indicated to the Russians that plans were in hand for an early landing. Kruschev gave way for the first time: he stopped twelve Russian ships before they entered the interception zone and he accepted UNO's proposal of a temporary suspension of activity. Two secret *messages* to Kennedy bore witness to his anxiety; in these he accepted dismantlement of the Soviet bases, the *quid pro quo* being the lifting of the blockade, an undertaking not to invade Cuba and the dismantlement of American bases in Turkey. Kennedy was now in a position of strength; he allowed several Soviet ships to get through but on 27 October he rejected Kruschev's proposals, gave assurances against any invasion of Cuba and demanded that dismantlement be supervised. On 28 October, the Pentagon *published* a list of reserve units called up for service and *declared* that 40,000 marines were ready to land. Kruschev finally accepted Kennedy's proposal. But Castro refused any supervisory measures; a compromise was finally reached on the basis of dismantlement of the Soviet bases in exchange for a promise that there would be no invasion of Cuba.

This first historical example of a bilateral deterrent manœuvre carried out in deadly earnest shows up the mechanics of the operation. Just as in the single combat of Homer's days, everything depends initially upon verbal *threats* reinforced by *significant gestures*. The declarations and gestures are designed to impress the enemy without necessarily producing an irrevocable situation: Kruschev stopped half his ships when the quarantine was announced, Kennedy let some Soviet ships through without searching them. The threats issued, and substantiated by concrete measures, were not fulfilled but they kept up the pressure: for instance, Kennedy assured Kruschev that he would not land in Cuba but the next day the Pentagon stated that 40,000 marines were ready to land. Like a well-schooled quadrille, when one advances the other retires but the first does not go too far and then the other advances in his turn.

The object is clearly not the defeat of the enemy but compromise; in other words, a solution in which the spoils are shared and limited by mutual concessions. This in fact is the great weakness of this strategy – it cannot guard against nibbling. Nevertheless it can – as it did in Cuba – correct an overventuresome situation without producing too serious risks.

The all-out case

The deterrent manœuvre may be played upon a wider keyboard of violence but the technique would be the same: far reaching threats, limited action designed to demonstrate determination in order to make the enemy give way and continuous search for a compromise. If the situation does not improve, a real, but as small as possible, step up the scale of escalation is taken, combined with declarations threatening the worst.

Cuba was played on the two lowest notes of the scale (statements and conventional hostile action), in other words at the cold war level but under the umbrella of the major mutual menace of nuclear holocaust. A more serious crisis might necessitate playing more highly pitched notes in the scale of violence, with the exception always of the topmost note, that of the 'spasm' nuclear exchange. If the assorted pressures of conventional hostile action were not enough, one would be forced to have recourse to limited conventional war, though keeping the buttons on the foils as long as possible. If one side then played its cards wrong and was faced with the necessity of averting rapid defeat, a few tactical nuclear explosions would be enough to bring the aggressor up short and would undoubtedly force the two sides to agree before crossing the final threshold. If, contrary to expectation, compromise was still impossible, the more courageous of the two – in other words the less frightened or the more foolhardy – would loose off a few strategic warning shots, initially perhaps into some empty space but then, if necessary, against military or civilian targets. If the worst came to the worst, this warning would evoke an equally limited reply and straight away the scale of destruction and the terror of their peoples would force the two sides into a compromise. This controlled regulated and calculated raising of the stakes has little in common with the spontaneous escalation so frequently pictured. It would be an implacable war of nerves, a hellish game conducted with a cool head, a terrible test of

73

will-power, so terrible that one can hardly imagine that it could be carried too far.

But might not one of the players lose his head? Might he not in a moment of panic let loose the 'spasm' strategic bombardment? This brings us back to the problem we discussed when dealing with escalation: unless someone goes mad – which cannot be completely excluded – a decision of this sort is only possible for the side possessing a counter-force capability sufficient to reduce the enemy's riposte to an acceptable level.

In the present situation between the two great nuclear powers this is highly improbable. It is for this reason that the Cuba game was played with such caution. For this reason too, if one day a serious crisis forced the two opponents to go up one or two notes on the keyboard of escalation, we can be sure that neither of them would go to the limit.

Thanks to nuclear deterrence, whatever may be the stake, the great nuclear war ought never to take place.

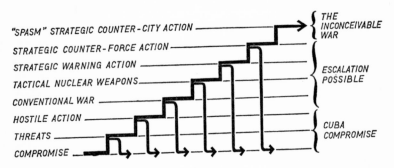

Conclusions

Stabilization or escalation are contagious phenomena linking the various levels of the use of force; we have seen their potentialities and their limitations. Because these links exist, deterrence forms a cohesive whole within which the object must be to make the best use of those forms of deterrence available at whatever level.

The art consists of combining the deterrent effect of threats of escalation with stabilizing security measures to ensure that escalation does not in fact take place: we have to preserve the ghoulish quality of the nuclear weapon but at the same time control it closely; we have to play the risks of escalation at the various levels, at the same time taking precautions against it; we have to stabilize that which may be dangerous, but at the same time preserve an element of risk.

In this situation of permanent contradiction, advantage must be taken of the natural bent of each of the levels: the nuclear level is that of the major threat and its presence, however small, – provided it is preserved – is enough to guarantee the peace; the conventional level must, in the first instance, stop up the cracks in the nuclear deterrent system which would otherwise allow minor or limited actions to take place; this level can also, however, by means of its tactical nuclear element, restore to the nuclear level a welcome risk of instability; the cold war level is that at which one can do almost anything without danger, but its deterrent effect may extend to all levels, so much so that it can neutralize a clear material superiority.

The deterrent manœuvre must, therefore, combine in judiciously measured quantities the apocalyptic threat, the checks and the military risks with moral or political inhibitions; it can thus weave the various levels into a close-knit network of measured and carefully confirmed threats, together with security safeguards, all of which will combine to paralyse the enemy while at the same time preserving our own freedom of action.

4 OVERALL CONCLUSIONS ON BILATERAL DETERRENCE

This is not yet the moment for conclusions, for the only true problem is not the bilateral but the multilateral. But at least we can, at this point, summarize the basic characteristics of the phenomenon of deterrence.

Deterrence has been brought to the fore by the nuclear level but it in fact turns out to be a phenomenon of general application with differing trends at each of the levels of action (stability at the nuclear level, instability at the conventional and cold war levels); it produces continuous interaction between the various levels and so can, within certain limits, modify their natural trends.

But this deterrent mechanism is governed by two basic contradictions:

1 Because once launched, the risk it involves is inevitable and mutual, the nuclear level is the only true deterrent level. But today this level is tending towards a dangerous stability, dangerous because this might stabilize its deterrent effect upon the other levels. Deterrent strategy must therefore be both highly intelligent and highly thoughtful; it must be applied to all levels and must be looked at as a whole; in particular it must preserve the risk of escalation.

2 The deterrent manœuvre, which relies upon fear of nuclear war, must also be based upon a refusal to contemplate nuclear war: nuclear war is no longer thinkable and none of those in a position to wage it accept it as a possibility. How therefore can the validity of its threat be maintained?

There have been three types of answer to this conundrum:

Make nuclear war once more a rational act by preserving or re-establishing so great a superiority (primarily through counter-force capacity) that only the loser would be faced with unacceptable losses;

Play upon the irrationality of a war of suicide in order to maintain fear of reaction or of escalation, both of which are always possible;

Humanize nuclear war by reducing its intensity to modest proportions.

None of these three answers alone appears really to fill the bill.

As usual, the solution appears to be that we must be ready to juggle with these three possibilities as best we can:

(1) Try to re-establish or appear to re-establish sufficient offensive superiority to make the nuclear threat rational;

(2) Failing this, cover up as far as possible by an attitude of irrationality;

(3) If, in spite of everything, we are forced to go to the use of nuclear weapons, humanize and limit the war as far as we can. This

is no particularly brilliant scheme but it does produce the essential minimum of flexibility.

For this reason, there is danger in dogmatic and rigid solutions such as those which refuse to accept any quest for offensive superiority, any irrationality or any humanization (Sokolovsky) or, on the other hand, plead for humanization during the deterrent phase (McNamara).

In deterrence strategy, as in all strategy, any solution may be the best possible in one set of circumstances and the worst conceivable in others.

Similarly deterrence cannot be based solely upon the nuclear weapon, for its deterrent capacity is inherently changeable, thus at once putting out of court any too black-and-white solution. The ideal in this business would be to achieve equilibrium at each of the levels, but that is not as a rule possible. One is therefore forced to try and achieve an overall equilibrium, superiority at one level compensating for inferiority at another. In order, however, to guard against a possible and more or less complete paralysis of the nuclear level, it is essential that conventional forces be adapted quickly to the role which has now become their primary task. This means that our conventional forces system must be capable of rapidly increasing their size and strength as circumstances demand. We shall be coming back to this question in Chapter Four.

Finally, however effective the deterrence, there will still be cracks in the system at the conventional and cold war levels. In particular the cold war level remains almost entirely unaffected by nuclear deterrence.

As a result, in the nuclear deterrence age, *action* is concentrated at the cold war level, reinforced sometimes by limited use of conventional force. Nuclear deterrence now plays no more than a negative limitation and security role. The positive game of strategy is now played through the pressure exerted by the minor forms of the use of force.

Three

Multilateral Deterrence

With the analysis of bilateral deterrence as a background, we can now make a start on the study of deterrence at its real level, the multilateral; we shall then at last be in a position to try to answer the main questions posed by present day strategy.

With this in view, I propose to follow the same step-by-step method used for bilateral deterrence: I shall first try to strip down the mechanism for multilateral deterrence; this I shall do by making a close analysis of the effect upon a bilateral nuclear situation of the presence of a third party, who is a *de facto* or *de jure* ally of one of the two principal opponents; then, based on the result of this analysis, I shall extrapolate to bring out the basic features of a system of deterrence when N parties are involved. Finally I shall try to deduce the resulting implications upon the value and the form of military alliances in the nuclear age and also upon the agonizing problem of proliferation.

This is inevitably a somewhat dry subject but it is of extreme importance.

1 THE PROBLEM OF THE THIRD PARTY

The problem of bilateral deterrence was no more than a working hypothesis used to simplify initial study of the phenomenon. The appearance within a deterrent system involving two great nuclear powers of a third party, assumed to be noticeably weaker than but allied to one of the principal opponents, brings us at once into a field governed by different laws; we are no longer dealing with a simple dialectic but with the combination of three dialectics operating simultaneously, the result of the action of any one of three parties upon any other.

To deal with this extremely complicated problem, we must first get quite clear what the third party's dialectic will be, the third party being assumed to be weak and faced with a powerful opponent. This in fact boils down to a special instance of simple bilateral deterrence, such as we have dealt with in the previous chapter. It is worth considering as a problem in itself, since, when considered purely from the bilateral angle, it has given rise to numerous misconceptions.

DIRECT EFFECT UPON THE OPPONENT

Taking only the third party's direct effect upon a more powerful opponent and discounting action by the third party's ally, the inevitable conclusion is that the stronger will deter the weaker. This can be proved as follows:

If the third party is much weaker than his opponent in nuclear weapons, his direct deterrent capability will depend upon his riposte capability as the previous chapter shows.[1] If this capability is greater than a certain percentage of the enemy resources (and it can be a very small percentage, 5 to 10 per cent for instance), his deterrent capability will still be appreciable at least so long as his more powerful opponent does not judge the stake to be considerably more important than this proportion of his own resources. But deterrence will also clearly depend upon the value of the stake in the eyes of the third party. If he is faced with an opponent of the size of the USSR or the United States, he risks destruction of more than 50 per cent of his resources and perhaps of something approaching 100 per cent. The only stake justifying suicide from his point of view would be complete loss of freedom—and even that is arguable: the disparity in the stakes can, therefore, lead to mutual deterrence on both sides, but if it is to do so, the stake must be total for the weaker party and minor for the stronger.

[1] See in Chapter Two, 'Study of Nuclear Stability'.

If to this initial balance sheet be added the unknown factor of the survival capacity of the third party's second strike resources, the conclusion must be that the dialectic between one very strong opponent and another very weak one must normally result in the weaker being deterred and the stronger having freedom of action, except in the extreme case when the weaker is threatened with a total loss of independence. The direct deterrence which the third party can achieve therefore depends almost entirely on his opponent's estimate of his determination to resort to a decision of desperation.

This conclusion, unarguable on the bilateral plane, has been at the root of the criticism levelled both in France and abroad at small independent striking forces. But, as we shall see presently, this criticism is somewhat elementary and is not valid in a multilateral context.

INFLUENCE OF THE THIRD PARTY UPON A SITUATION OF EQUILIBRIUM BETWEEN TWO GREAT POWERS

This influence is the key to multilateral deterrence. In fact the dialectic between two major opponents produces a somewhat specialized situation of equilibrium, analysed at length in the previous chapter. *The results of the intrusion of a third party must be evaluated in the light of this equilibrium.*

Features of bilateral deterrence in a situation of relative equilibrium

As soon as two major opponents are in a state of relative equilibrium (in other words, as soon as the response capability of each is an object of apprehension for the other) both are afraid of getting into a situation in which they would be forced to destroy each other. Therefore, as we have seen when dealing with bilateral deterrence, both will adopt a very delicately shaded policy in order to avoid calling in question any stake too important from the other's point of view. If, through accident or error of judgment on the part of one of them, a crisis occurs, they will do their best to settle it at the

80

lowest cost, if possible by threats but if action is necessary by something very limited. If in the end the situation becomes so serious that they are forced to give proof of their determination to use nuclear weapons in the ultimate issue, this will be done at the lowest possible level of violence and in very moderate stages in order at all times to keep open the possibility of resolving the crisis by compromise.

This attitude of caution–which we saw in full operation in the case of Cuba–does not spring from any lack of determination but from an acute realization of the enormous risks involved in the nuclear situation.

In such a situation, adequately stable but uneasy, it is very difficult for one of the major parties to exert any credible deterrent effect in defence of interests which the other party knows to be marginal in his opponent's eyes.

There are in fact areas of marginal interest but they are unlikely to be of the same degree of value to both sides. In cases where these interests would appear to be low level for one side–and therefore from his point of view would not justify a major risk–and more important for the other side, the latter may be tempted to blackmail his way to crisis level. If then his opponent shows greater determination than he had reckoned, the crisis may assume dangerous proportions unless the side which took the initiative withdraws. This is what happened in Berlin and Cuba. But in both cases the crisis stemmed from a mistaken appreciation of the other side's determination.

In short, and to conclude, a bilateral situation between two major nuclear powers characterized by relative equilibrium and by caution, still leaves certain zones of instability which may give rise to new formidable trials of strength.

The intervention of a third party

This picture may be fundamentally modified by the intervention of a third nuclear party if the third party is located in or has important interests in a threatened zone but one which is marginal for the two principals.

(1) From the point of view of the third party, the zone is vital and not marginal.

(2) If his interests are threatened, he may react by measures which, limited though they may be, may risk causing the principals' game to overstep the limits of prudence they consider necessary; he could thus ruin any hope of a compromise based upon a progressively ascending scale of threat.

These are two vital points and their effects must be weighed carefully. The effects will differ according to whether the balance of forces between the two principals gives a definite superiority of response to one of them or whether there is a relative parity of nuclear risk between the two.

Case when the ally of the third party is the stronger

If the third party's ally has a definite superiority of riposte (in other words, a first strike sufficient to reduce the enemy riposte to an acceptable level), his opponent may threaten but definitely cannot take any risk of provoking him to launch the first strike, which he would do if the other side were to try to destroy the third party by preventive attack. *In this case, therefore, the third party's nuclear force is automatically protected by the existence of his ally's force,* irrespective of his own survival capability.

On the other hand if, in reply to a threat, the third party were to respond by hostilities, nuclear or not, there are only two courses open to his opponent: either he must relax his pressure or he must let loose his first strike against the more powerful ally in order as far as possible to reduce the latter's riposte. The second alternative is highly improbable in view of the extent of the destruction which he would himself suffer.

In this case, therefore, *the existence of the third party means that his interests are directly linked to those of his ally.* That which, in the eyes of the enemy, might seem to be a marginal zone becomes of critical importance. Conversely, whatever may be his own true interests, the more powerful ally is compelled to consider the interests of the third party as if they were his own.

Case when the opponent of the third party is the stronger

If it is the opponent of the third party who possesses superiority of riposte, the threat the latter can exert becomes very much more serious, since he must under no circumstances be placed in a position where he feels obliged to fire first. Reactions must therefore be more cautious and more precisely calculated. The fact remains, however, that neither of the two principals can actually wish to initiate a major conflict over interests which, in the final analysis, are to them secondary.

In this situation, the determination of the third party creates a major danger for the two principals: his opponent cannot launch a preventive nuclear attack upon the third party without giving the latter's ally an opportunity of being the first to fire and so finding his own riposte reduced; equally, he will not start by attacking the other principal because he does not wish to initiate the great holocaust. On his side the third party's ally will be only too well aware of the major danger of such a conflict and will try to avert it by urging compromise. In short, even in this case, *everything will take place as if the interests of the third party had become those of his ally.*

Because of the risks involved in resistance by the third party, the relative instability between the two principals will result in stabilization of the marginal zone defended by the third party.

Case of equilibrium between the two principals

If there is stable equilibrium between the two principals, in other words if on each side the destructive capacity of the riposte is unacceptable (the present situation), the influence of the third party is still just as great. In fact in this case the probability of either of the two principals intervening with nuclear weapons is very small, if not non-existent; but the danger to them both will be so great that they are bound to avoid aggravating the conflict in any way, lest the intervention of the third party risk inflaming it beyond the tolerable limits of security.

Let us look at various hypotheses illustrating this situation.

(1) The alliance between one of the two principals and the third party is a close one. The enemy will be able to do no more than make play with various shades of threat to test the solidarity between the allies. The major ally has merely to give a declaration of support to put an end to this game.

(2) The alliance is less close and the interests of the two allies are clearly divergent on the matter at issue. The enemy may hope to make play with this divergence and may try either a threat backed by force, or even action using limited force. Open resistance by the third party will then produce a situation of extreme danger, because of the risk of escalation. The third party's ally, who may have been hesitant up to this point, can do no other than intervene in order to resolve the crisis.

(3) The allies are completely split as regards the object of the conflict and the third party's ally declares himself neutral in this case. Even under this hypothesis, the third party still has a chance of being supported by his former ally, *provided he resists, holds on firmly and can throughout keep up a threat of escalation.* He will then, in effect, face the two major opponents with an international problem of a most serious nature, unacceptable to both of them. The former ally will be forced to intervene, either lining up behind the third party or more probably putting an end to the conflict by insisting on a compromise.

On the other hand, if the third party is rapidly defeated, the *fait accompli* must be accepted. An important point therefore is the length of time for which the third party can keep up his resistance and his nuclear threat. To guard against this possibility it is essential that the third party should possess conventional forces equipped with tactical nuclear weapons and that his small striking force should have a good survival capability. These two conditions should be noted in passing since we shall be coming back to them later.

CONCLUSIONS

The intrusion of a third party into a situation of bipolar nuclear equilibrium therefore has strategic consequences out of all proportion to the nuclear strength of the third party.

84

(1) The third party's vital interests become directly linked to those of his more powerful ally.

(2) The enemy cannot ignore the third party, nor can he make any error of judgment as regards either the solidarity between the two allies or the importance to the principal ally of those zones which may be marginal for him but are vital for the third party.

(3) In the event of crisis, the existence of the third party means that the more powerful ally need only become involved as a seconder.

(4) These implications are basically deterrent in their effect and so contribute to strategic stability.

Some analysts have tried to summarize the role of the third party in two words: suicide or blackmail. This description is both superficial and tendentious; the truth, as has just been made clear, is far more complex. Moreover, the whole problem of the deterrent phenomenon becomes distorted each time a nuclear problem is considered from the point of view of launching an attack and not from that of deterrence – two diametrically opposed things.[1]

Response to any aggression by strategic bombardment amounts to suicide. It could only result from a remarkably oversimplified concept in which the threat of the launching of an attack was confused with the launching itself. We shall see later the varying lights and shades inherent in this problem.

Blackmail is a nasty word, loosely used to describe something which in fact happens all the time in international politics: everyone is trying to make his own interests prevail, using the means available to him. If certain means prove to be extremely powerful, there is no need to be ashamed of them nor to consider them as dishonest. Other people would be quite prepared to use them if they had them.

In fact *the effect of the existence of a third party is to restrict to some extent the freedom of action of the two principals.* The supporters of a bipolar system consider this a disproportionate result, all the more so since it is achieved with very limited forces. Worse still, the idea has been put forward that the third party might be able to initiate a nuclear conflict; that has been considered unacceptable as being

[1] For this reason the oversimplified theory known as the 'trip-wire' is not even worth discussing. No one wants to initiate a nuclear conflict.

85

too dangerous and removing from the principal players their right to 'decide on peace and war'.

These are major errors of thinking which cannot be dealt with lightly; they are serious enough to justify the detailed examination which now follows.

2 THE PROBLEM OF NUCLEAR ALLIANCES

OBJECTIONS TO INDEPENDENT NUCLEAR FORCES

Confusion of theory is invariably exemplified by a series of contradictory statements. When towards 1946 the Soviet Union realized the existence of the nuclear danger, they proclaimed at one and the same time that the nuclear weapon was ineffective against the USSR, that it was capable of destroying humanity and must therefore be done away with. Similarly when, towards 1961, the American analysts discovered that a third party in the nuclear game might be a major factor in the development of a conflict, they stated publicly, first that the third party would play no role (giving reasons based on bilateral deterrence), and secondly that the existence of more than two centres of decision (one in each camp) would constitute an unacceptable danger to peace; they concluded that it was essential to keep deterrence within a strictly bilateral framework.

Here it is enough to note that the conclusion reached in both cases proved that the reality of the risk had been recognized.

Mr McNamara combined all these contradictions in his wellknown phrase that a small independent nuclear force would be at once 'ineffective, useless and dangerous'.

Ineffectiveness

'Ineffective?' In the first part of this chapter, we have seen that this is not so in the case of multilateral deterrence. In any case, how can it be said that a force is both dangerous and ineffective, when danger is in fact basic to deterrence?

86

Uselessness

The term 'useless' could only really be justified if the force was in fact 'ineffective'. But it is quite clear what is really meant – the effectiveness of the United States nuclear force is adequate for deterrence; that is true in general terms but may not be true in the case of interests which are marginal from the United States' point of view. On this point attempts have been made in various quarters to bring up the delicate subject of confidence in the given word of an ally. This uselessly exacerbated the discussion by introducing an argument upon which there can be no conclusion and which is difficult to discuss without raising passions – rather like the gentleman who tried to prove that God existed by giving his word of honour that He did exist . . . From an objective point of view, however, the following two points are relevant:

(1) The NATO treaty lays down that aggression against one of the members shall be considered as aggression against all (here is the given word), but that the form of support to be given to the State subject to aggression shall be left to the decision of each ally; (here is the real significance of the given word).

(2) In the case of the United States, the fact that she has thus reserved her freedom of decision particularly on the employment of nuclear weapons, implies that she envisages the possibility of not using her nuclear forces in certain circumstances, even for instance, though her conventional forces might be engaged.

In the light of our analysis of the nuclear risk, the American position is perfectly understandable; let it be stated at once that France would act similarly in a similar situation. It does not imply that we are questioning the word of an ally, but simply that nuclear war is something too serious to be linked automatically to any definite situation.

What then remains of the alliance? One French author has stated that this situation justifies the deduction that in the nuclear age alliances no longer have meaning: the magnitude of the danger outweighs any sense of solidarity. This is clearly an exaggeration, based to a large extent upon an inaccurate appreciation of the nature of nuclear deterrence.

This pessimistic view about alliances would appear to be confirmed by a phenomenon repeated throughout history: whenever a nation considers that it is in too great danger as a result of the links binding it to its ally, it has withdrawn from the alliance (e.g. Munich, Dunkirk, the 1940 armistice, the Italian surrender, etc. to quote only last war instances). If such situations were to recur, they would produce the same effects and that should be no cause for surprise. The new question before us today is whether in fact the nuclear risks are now permanently so great that the whole basis of any alliance is changed.

That nuclear risks may be deadly is indisputable and this is the reason given for stating that alliances are at an end. But *nuclear deterrence lies not in the actual employment of nuclear weapons but simply in the utilization of their threat* and, as we have seen, it is difficult to keep this threat credible because of the stability of the nuclear situation. The threat only retains a certain validity in spite of its very small degree of probability thanks to the magnitude of the risk and the subtle procedures used to preserve for it a minimum of credibility. In the situation of nuclear stability already reached it would be surprising if a highly unlikely, though very large-scale, risk was enough to make anyone give up without more ado interests which he considered vital.

This brings us back to the problem of common interests and of their importance, sometimes vital, sometimes secondary and sometimes marginal for one or other of the allies. If one or more allies have vital common interests, their alliance will be a solid one and they will be ready to take considerable risks together (nevertheless, even in this case the alliance will not be proof against every situation and if one of the allies finds himself in extreme danger he will break away). If, on the other hand, the common interests in question are of insufficient importance from the point of view of one of the allies, the slightest risk of conflict may destroy the solidarity of the alliance. This picture of alliances is nothing new but the existence of the nuclear weapon tends to show it up in much sharper outline.

88

Alliances are not dead—we see that every day—but they may well prove more unstable.

Paradoxically, and contrary to the majority of present day doctrines *the only method of giving them greater stability is to base an alliance upon independent nuclear forces*: interests which are vital for the weaker allies but marginal for the stronger then become vital for the latter as well and so solidarity becomes more complete.

Danger

This produces a new problem and it is of prime importance: how can an ally be expected to accept what to him are exorbitant risks occasioned by a conflict which he considers marginal? How can he be expected to bind himself 'till death us do part' to a partner whose initiatives may bring him to ruin? This is Mr McNamara's third word, the 'danger' of independent forces.

What is the nature of the danger created by an independent nuclear force? Obviously it is the risk that the third party may react unwisely to a threat and may thereby give rise either to serious misunderstanding between the two principals or even to the *fait accompli* of open and irrevocable hostilities precluding any compromise solution. The fear is that the third party may play the game badly.

It is clear for instance that if, during the Cuba crisis, Great Britain had arrested Soviet ships at the moment when Kennedy was letting them through unsearched, the delicate shade of pressure which the United States wished to exert would have been fundamentally affected. The false note thus struck would have been much more serious if the incident had involved seizure of Soviet rockets in transit. Similarly if Federal Germany or France were to initiate radical retaliatory measures during a period of tension in Berlin, any incident might quickly cause the game to transgress the limits of security considered necessary and produce a situation impossible to sort out. These examples show that the problem of the third party presents itself long before there is any question of nuclear weapons being used and that therefore close coordination from the cold war level upwards is a present day necessity. *A fortiori* it is completely indispensable at the nuclear level; that is obvious. This is the essential basis of those doctrines which urge complete integration of nuclear forces under a single command.

The problem of coordination of independent nuclear forces has so far been considered from too narrow a point of view: people have not been willing to admit the real advantages which might accrue from the existence of a number of centres of decision; they have not really looked to see whether there is not some satisfactory solution in the field of nuclear coordination similar to that into which we have been forced at the other levels. But this coordination is perfectly possible. Why should it be supposed that the third party's reactions will be more irresponsible at the nuclear level than at the other levels? Why should it be pretended that he will act less intelligently when his behaviour involves greater danger, not only for others, but for himself?

In fact this anxiety arises primarily because nuclear doctrines at present seem to diverge. This being so, the fear is that independence might lead to ill-judged manœuvres, all the more serious because the third party has the necessary resources literally to set a match to the powder barrel, even though he would be the first to go up in flames, also because the irrational attitude adopted for deterrence purposes throws doubt upon his judgment.

This situation is neither fortuitous nor inevitable. It results from the fact that up to now nuclear problems have been studied and aired within a strictly national framework, because of the United States attitude and the MacMahon Act; if since the formation of NATO the Americans had been prepared to share with their allies the facts behind the nuclear strategy they were developing, all members of NATO would have moved forward together and would today have reached the same level of understanding of the phenomenon – which is not the case now. There would of course still be differences of appreciation as a result of divergencies of interest. But let it be repeated, the problem would be no different in nature from that facing us at the cold war level. The 'danger' of independent nuclear forces stems solely from the fact that the allies are at different stages in their interpretation of nuclear problems.

To remove this differentiation the only solution is to get the allies to study and work in concert on the complex problems raised by the existence of nuclear weapons—as they should have done for the last ten years; they must do so not only on the technical level but, more important, on the highest politico-strategic level. Only along these lines can the mutual education of the partners in the alliance be achieved and only thus can they be brought to understand the real common interests of the alliance at the nuclear level.

In the international as in the internal political field, true democracy depends on education. By trying to use integration as a method of preserving full control over all nuclear forces, the Americans tend to perpetuate and increase the present difference in the degree of understanding reached by the various allies. Yet if it is desired to ensure that a third party's actions will invariably take into account the very strict conditions governing the nuclear confrontation of two great powers, that third party must be treated unreservedly as an ally; the various aspects of the situation with which he may be confronted must be discussed with him thoroughly, without dogmatism and without reservations on the score of nuclear secrecy (a futile business anyway); a real common strategic doctrine would thus be built up collectively. This exercise would take time, for the new nuclear realities can only be grasped after a long period of incubation; but it would be surprising if it did not eventually lead to mutual understanding of the differing points of view and the evolvement of the most advantageous policy for all concerned.

Then we should have produced not some integrated force (such as the Multilateral Force) attempting by subterfuge to preserve the appearance of autonomy for each ally, nor a disunited collection of unequal and mistrustful partners, but a *real championship team*, ready to play the deterrence game in all its delicacy and using all the most intelligent manœuvres. The essential coordination would not be achieved by handing over power of allied decision on nuclear matters to one member nor by a veto system, which is quite unacceptable, but through full knowledge of what is in the collective interest. Our common enemy would be placed in a far more difficult position and the possibility of deterrence would be greatly increased.

This conclusion will have to be reached sooner or later, for it is the only practicable one; it has two important corollaries:

First, that the third party must be quite clear that he must play his part within the overall framework and that any independent action he takes must be designed to support and complement the action of his ally, that his object must be to achieve maximum deterrence and avoid any situation liable to get out of control. *He must conduct his manœuvre with an eye just as much upon the ally whose deterrent power he is using as upon the enemy he wishes to deter.* Independence must not be tantamount to blind egoism;

Secondly, the only way in which an independent force can avoid being 'dangerous' is to be truly allied, since only thus is it possible to conceive of proper coordination, so essential once the resources are there.

Conclusion

I have gone into the objections to an independent nuclear force in detail in order to dispose of the somewhat instinctive prejudice on which these objections are almost invariably based and to get the problem back into its true perspective.

It is amusing to note that the American reaction against nuclear forces of which they are not in full control has been very similar to the European reaction *vis-à-vis* the Americans at the beginning of the nuclear age: people were scared of the possible danger because they questioned the wisdom of the possessors of these new weapons. Since then we have learnt that the possession of nuclear weapons produces a reassuring sense of responsibility. The Americans will find the same in their turn.

In any case criticism aimed at preventing nuclear polycentrism is no longer a live issue. Even if polycentrism is not a good thing, it is happening. All we can do is to take what advantage we can of it.

POSSIBLE ADVANTAGES OF NUCLEAR ALLIANCES

Since I seem to have got involved in the business of de-mystifying the bogey of so-called independent nuclear forces, it is now up to me to show first why I believe that criticism is generally ill-founded, and secondly that there is a very definite balance of advantage in favour of these forces.

Solidarity

The first point in their favour has already been touched on in passing: by their very existence independent nuclear forces produce a basic solidarity between allies, necessarily covering the whole range of their vital interests. This is a fundamental point; the resulting solidarity is stronger than all written undertakings; an enemy cannot therefore play upon the differences of interest which always exist between allies on one point or another.

This solidarity is not dangerous, as some people have tried to make out; its basic advantage is that it acts as a deterrent, in other words it prevents an enemy thinking that he can make play with certain incidents in which he might have hoped to see one of the allies accept a compromise behind the back of the other. *The existence of independent nuclear forces tends to reduce the area in which the cold war can operate.*

But this solidarity does more: instead of merely giving rise to a measure of deterrence, as has often been stated, it *forces* the nuclear powers to agree among themselves and to follow a concerted line of action. In this respect its influence is so great that it has forced even the main opponents themselves to take certain precautions (such as the 'hot line') against possible misunderstandings.

Team work and uncertainty for the enemy

Solidarity also means that a more effective form of deterrent manœuvre is possible: in bilateral strategy each of the opponents keeps his eye on the other's determination and gears his reactions accordingly. In multilateral strategy the fact of being faced by several opponents makes any appreciation of the situation extraordinarily complicated, so much so that it may make any forecast impossible.

With three parties involved there are fifteen possible ways in

93

which the three participants can come into play.[1] At each level each of the parties may intervene in a different manner and there are, say, at least ten to fifteen possibilities (warnings, partial mobilization, economic measures, blockade, various military measures, etc.). Working this out it will be found that the number of typical solutions soon passes the two hundred mark. If four parties are involved the same method of calculation produces a figure of well over a thousand.

Using the electronic computers available nowadays planning of this nature is not outside the bounds of possibility; it is quite clear, however, that the side which *concerts* its actions has a considerable advantage over a single opponent; the latter will be faced with complete *uncertainty* both as to the probable effect of his own actions and even as to the degree of coordination or freedom of initiative of each of the parties he is facing. Taking into account the imponderables of this highly complicated game it is clear that any forecast of success is increasingly problematical and that therefore *the situation is far more stable than if only two opponents are involved.*

Possibility of technical osmosis

The stability and solidarity achieved by the existence of independent nuclear forces would result in a form of relationship between allies which has hitherto proved impossible (apart from that between Great Britain and the United States resulting from the close links existing between them when the atomic weapon was invented).

In fact if a certain proliferation of nuclear weapons were ultimately accepted as advantageous, the main objections to the exchange of technical information would lose much of their validity. It might then be that expenditure on research could be used more rationally and in the general interest instead of the wasteful process of today, at which future historians will inevitably raise their eyebrows.[2]

---

[1] Based on the various possibilities of initiative by the three parties (six ways) and the various possibilities of riposte to these initiatives (fifteen ways).

[2] The fact that an ally can refuse to his partners technical secrets which the enemy already knows, serves only to underline yet again the *de facto* solidarity between the nuclear powers.

Conclusion

The foregoing arguments show that instead of anathematizing independent nuclear forces it would be better to accommodate oneself to this new situation, which is going to arise anyway, and to make the most of the real possibilities it could offer, *if we knew how to use them.*

We shall then realize that this continuous insistence on complete integration of nuclear forces stems from instinctive prejudice and from too one-sided a view of the problem of multilateral deterrence; moreover, quite apart from the fact that integration was impossible politically, even if it had succeeded it would have meant that we were denying ourselves a definite strategic advantage.

I fear however that this conclusion is unlikely to be acceptable yet awhile . . .

This having been said, I do not pretend that in practice a multipolar nuclear system is necessarily the best. That will depend basically upon the skill with which it is used and upon the formation of an adequately coordinated team. The multilateral problem, however, brings us back to that same paradox which governs the bilateral problem: the nuclear weapon is beneficial only if we succeed both in maintaining the validity of its threat and in avoiding having to use it.

3 THE PROBLEM OF NUCLEAR PROLIFERATION

If an increase in the number of nuclear powers enhances stability, must we not then admit that as wide as possible a spread of nuclear weapons is desirable?

Reasons for proliferation

Certain writers—on both sides of the Atlantic—have put forward this theory, some because in fact they think that proliferation will come anyway, others because they ascribe to any nuclear capability, even a small one, an inherent and total power of bilateral deterrence. The idea, though in a sense theoretical, is interesting: since the

95

nuclear weapon makes war impossible, by having it everywhere one should achieve a completely static international system: the nuclear weapon would thus become a sort of anti-war vaccine.

This somewhat extreme concept should be compared – despite the basic difference between it and a multiplicity of decision-making centres – to the 1952 policy, known as that of MC 70, under which the United States decided to provide all their allies with some nuclear armament. In fact, in the light of the views of the time on the possibility of aggression, what this policy did was to set up in sensitive areas a perfectly obvious machine for spontaneous escalation, the object being to deter the enemy from any temptation to nibble. It is true that the United States kept jealous control over these weapons but it was clear that, apart from local incidents, they would not have been able to forbid their use. A broader basis was therefore given to deterrence by means of dissemination of nuclear weapons. It was not until four years later that the majority of American theorists, haunted by the danger that nuclear war then represented for the United States, concluded that the safety catch must be put on this machinery for escalation by highly developed security measures.

On the technical side, moreover, many scientists believe that in a few years' time evolution will have made the production of nuclear energy so simple that, as far as cost is concerned, nuclear armaments will be within reach of the majority of countries. This 'democratization' of the nuclear weapon would *ipso facto* mean a widespread proliferation. Let it be said at once, however, that this is no prospect for the immediate future, that it is probably linked to the discovery of a method of controlling the fusion process and that even then all the experts do not accept it. The fact remains, however, that the possibility of technical developments facilitating a wide spread of nuclear weapons is a point worth careful consideration.

Dangers of nuclear proliferation

This possibility is generally held to be one fraught with danger.

How in fact could we rely upon the judgment of an increasing number of statesmen, very few of whom would be qualified to shoulder so crushing a responsibility? The possibility of a madman being around is of course obvious, but more likely—and therefore more disturbing—is the possibility simply of lack of judgment: problems of peace and war have now become too subtle to be understood by every politician whom chance may bring to power; persistence of the traditional notions about war, now completely obsolete, must inevitably lead to frightful catastrophes. The risk might be acceptable if these catastrophes could be localized; but the power of nuclear weapons is infinitely variable and will become more so as they are miniaturized. The amusing story of the film *The Mouse that Roared* might well therefore come true in a big way and provide methods of blackmail on a scale totally unacceptable in international relations. In short, nuclear proliferation quite clearly opens up most disturbing prospects.

American analysts have frequently presented this problem in mathematical terms—the 'Nth Power Problem'. This method of presentation distorts the true nature of the question; it is basically qualitative, not quantitative.

In fact, as we have seen, the existence of independent but co-ordinated nuclear forces has certain advantages as regards stabilization. It may also be accepted that the existence of independent but uncoordinated forces might prove useful and would not produce any additional dangers, provided they were in the possession of peaceful and sensible countries like Switzerland, Sweden or Holland. It would be very different though, in the case of Cuba, the UAR, or Indonesia. Moreover, in unstable countries there can be no guarantee of the wisdom of whatever party might come to power.

The stability provided by the nuclear weapon is attainable only between *reasonable powers*. Boxes of matches should not be given to children.

Methods of limitation

This quick run over the course shows that *proliferation of nuclear weapons must under all circumstances be stopped sooner or later*, and at latest when the prospect of 'democratization' of nuclear weapons appears imminent.

This conclusion has been the basis of the attempts by the United

G

States and the USSR to preserve their present quasi-monopoly in nuclear matters. The agreement between them on the nuclear test ban was made with precisely this object in view. The effect of this first attempt to solve the problem will be to reduce the number of members of the nuclear club but it will not prevent a certain spread of nuclear weapons, primarily because tension between the US and the USSR is too great for them really to act in concert. The initial increases in the number of nuclear powers will take place under very difficult conditions and will therefore necessarily be limited to those nations sufficiently rich and imbued with sufficient determination to carry the thing through. There will therefore be a first small clutch of nuclear powers of very unequal strength and, as pointed out above, within each camp they will inevitably organize themselves to co-operate in the manner best suited to get the maximum benefit from the stability which the nuclear weapon can gain for them.

During this period the only difficult problem is that with which the USSR will be faced by China because – rightly or wrongly – people are still wondering how 'reasonable' China's political philosophy is.

Then may come the anticipated technical development bringing about a possible 'democratization' of the nuclear weapon. This development should be foreseeable several years ahead, since the process between invention and implementation will be slow. Since the danger is already on the horizon, we can be reasonably sure that it will evoke some very powerful defensive reactions.

Would total nuclear disarmament be a solution to this problem? Many people think so but they could not be more wrong: it would lose us the enormous advantage of the high degree of stability guaranteed by these weapons. Before the advent of nuclear weapons our century had seen two world conflicts of cataclysmic proportions, fatal for Europe; it is thanks to the nuclear weapon that so far we have not had a third, even more devastating. Our problem is not how to get rid of these weapons, for they are now indissolubly bound up with the fate of the modern world. Progress in this sense would imply technical retreat and that is impossible. The probability is that we are moving not towards nuclear disarmament but towards control of nuclear weapons.

98

I say this because the chances are that the danger will become so serious and so pressing that it will transcend in importance the conflicts of interest and doctrine which now keep the nuclear powers at odds. It is a pretty safe bet that at the latest when this happens, the nuclear powers will close their ranks in face of this common danger and will be forced to conclude between themselves a control agreement which they will not hesitate to enforce, more or less politely, on the rest of the world. *The threat of major proliferation will probably force the major nuclear powers to act in concert.* This concert will be a real one and will play a major role in the conduct of world affairs.

The more distant future

It is worth letting one's imagination run riot a little further in order to try and forecast subsequent evolution. There are, of course, too many unknown factors for anyone to think that he can foresee what will really happen. But at least one can try to guess the direction in which this shrunken interdependent world, built on the new foundations of our scientific-technical civilization is moving. The nuclear weapon and other means of mass destruction has given man exaggerated power; it will increasingly inhibit his tendency to gratify his lust for blood. Man's initiative will be canalized by this terrible disproportionate degree of power and in the long run it must inevitably reawaken his conscience and lead to the organization of a collective nuclear force as the secular arm of a true world authority.

This may seem a far distant utopian vision. It must not be built up into a naïve idyllic picture, for conflicts of interests, races and doctrines will persist and we know that civil wars are more terrible than foreign wars. Nevertheless this must be the final aim of that evolution in which the discovery of nuclear fission has inexorably involved us.

As we stand at the threshold of this new stage of human development the inscrutable sphinx of history is asking us the question whether we have the good sense to reach our goal gradually and by peaceful means or whether we shall do so through monstrous and grievous upheavals.

4 OVERALL CONCLUSIONS ON MULTILATERAL DETERRENCE

We are now in a position to draw conclusions on the overall problem of multilateral deterrence; although with so involved a subject caution is obviously required, I do so in the feeling that we have brought to light a number of proven facts and in the light of these we can either accept or reject some of the strategic solutions which have been put forward.

GENERAL CHARACTERISTICS OF MULTILATERAL DETERRENCE

The existence of a multilateral nuclear system produces an additional risk of instability and this restores to the nuclear level the deterrent capacity which, in a bilateral situation, tends to disappear as soon as the forces reach a certain degree of nuclear equilibrium. This mutual risk produces a high degree of *interdependence* between nuclear powers; it considerably increases deterrent capacity, to the point at which the opponents are restricted to extremely delicate action and their allies find difficulty in playing any game other than a closely coordinated one. The result is an entirely new degree of *stability*, covering the whole range of vital interests of the nuclear powers.

The effect of this *de facto* interdependence and solidarity within a nuclear alliance is to increase the mutual *influence* of the various allies, even though there may be great disparity of forces; within the alliance there will therefore be a great degree of equality.

But the stability of the effects of deterrence together with community of risk very definitely *reduce the freedom of action of the partners outside the limits of cold war*. In the nuclear age there is no longer any such thing as complete or even wide freedom of action, however great the theoretical autonomy of the forces concerned. Within an alliance *highly developed coordination* is a necessity, both to ensure that the common game is effectively played and also in the direct interest of each of the players.

This is a very different situation from the hopes often expressed both in the United States and France about safeguarding the maximum degree of national independence by means of nuclear forces. On the contrary, because of the gravity of the consequences it may produce and the seriousness of the responsibility thereby laid upon the nuclear powers, the nuclear weapon restricts their field of initiative even at the conventional level. For this reason, for instance, Indonesia can attack Malaysia or Algeria can attack Morocco. The United States or France could hardly do so. Entry into the nuclear club confers upon its members the guarantee that their vital interests will be taken fully into consideration both by their allies and their enemies but at the same time it *ipso facto* denies them that innocent irresponsibility which previously led them to think that they were masters of the decision 'for peace or war'.

In the nuclear world peace and war have lost their traditional meaning because nuclear war has become unthinkable and peace is nothing but the permanent interplay of deterrence. It is for this reason that fears about independent nuclear forces possibly 'triggering off' nuclear war are totally unrealistic. Such forces reinforce deterrence instead of reducing its effectiveness.

As far as the mechanism of deterrence is concerned, we have now seen that in a multilateral setting the deterrent qualities of the various levels in some cases differ considerably as compared with those they possessed in a bilateral system:

(a) Thanks to the existence of independent and allied nuclear forces the nuclear level can more easily recapture a sound deterrent capacity and this gives it greater influence over the conventional level. As a result the size of conventional forces can be kept very small, always provided that stability is reinforced by tactical nuclear weapons. This does not, however, eliminate the necessity for making plans possibly to increase conventional forces, should the nuclear deterrent lose its effectiveness:

(b) The cold war level still remains unaffected by the general deterrent influence of the nuclear level but the nuclear risk inherent in a multilateral system reduces the geographical zone in which cold war actions can take place by putting out of court those areas directly covered by the various nuclear forces. Conversely, the deterrent effect exerted upon the nuclear level by the cold war level is increased because the nuclear level is more unstable. Overall, general stability is greater.

THE MAJOR CONSEQUENCES

Strategically the foregoing conclusions clearly confirm the potential usefulness of independent nuclear forces both for the countries which own them and for their allies—in spite of present day reservations on the subject. In fact they automatically make allied solidarity applicable to all sufficiently important interests of all members of a nuclear alliance, and they tend to equalize the influence exerted by the various members within the alliance. They increase deterrent effect upon the enemy by demonstrating to him the degree of solidarity achieved and by increasing his uncertainty of the possible results of any aggressive action. They therefore reduce the size of the area in which the cold war can be pursued.

In short theoretical analysis leads to the conclusion that independent nuclear forces should contribute to general stability *always provided that the threat of these forces is not used in an irresponsible manner and without regard for the very strict rules governing the nuclear game.* Voluntary coordination is an absolute prerequisite if a multiplicity of centres of decision is to produce greater stability; but this voluntary coordination can only be achieved if concepts and forecasts are worked out communally.

If this proviso is met, the considerable effort at present being made by France to provide herself with an independent nuclear force, whatever its technical level may be, may prove of benefit not only to France but to the alliance. The alliance must sooner or later turn to account the advantages of a situation which it cannot prevent and with which it must simply learn to live. Moreover, thinking back to the prospect of a future 'concert of nuclear powers' to which reference was made, it may be that Europe as a whole will reap the advantages of the trail blazed by France and Great Britain, always provided that Europe has contrived to make adequate progress towards unity.

The multipolar world now forming will undoubtedly be a world with more than two centres of nuclear decision. This situation is not catastrophic; in fact it is the reverse; but it must not be confused with proliferation, which will undoubtedly be prevented as being too dangerous. Moreover it must be admitted that *for a long time to come this nuclear polycentrism will be hedged round by the bipolarity of the two major nuclear powers* which form the core of the deterrence system.

Finally, in a world stabilized by nuclear deterrence the elbow room for initiative in the use of force by any one nation will be considerably reduced. With the military potentials in equilibrium, attempts to bring about the inevitable changes can only be made via the minor crises resulting from indirect strategy.

As far as concepts go, it is clear that we are still cutting our first teeth in the nuclear age. New ideas are emerging gradually as we grope our way forward but in general we are still a long way from an overall understanding of the phenomenon.

The main difficulty lies in the persistence of obsolete concepts: it is very difficult not to look at things through the spectacles of the last war, adding the nuclear weapon as an adjunct. Even recognizing that such an attitude is nonsense, one is instinctively tempted to cudgel one's brains to make a picture of the course of a nuclear war and to guard against 'faulty' use of the new weapon. But there is no such thing as a 'correct' employment of them: *the role of the nuclear weapon is not to make war but to prevent it.* Unless we start from there, we shall inevitably go wrong.

But to prevent the catastrophe the threat must remain credible; there must therefore still be a risk and it must be carefully safeguarded. This contradiction is the essential key to the new age which seems, as it were, to carry within it both the power conferred on man and the safeguards to prevent him abusing it.

If this is so, it would seem that with the nuclear weapon nature has reproduced a collective counterpart to individual pain, a preserver of life through suffering for the living. The nuclear danger might therefore be a piece of natural machinery whose destiny is to prevent groups of human beings using their power for destruction beyond a certain level of violence; that would at least be a step towards a more peaceful, or rather a less cruelly insensible, world.

Part Two

The Consequences of Deterrence

The object of Part One was to set out the mechanics and the laws peculiar to deterrence. I now propose to try and deduce its main consequences. I shall deal first with the strictly military field; my object here is to discover some logical basis for the military system of the nuclear age. I shall then turn to the strategic field and hope to show the influence of strategic thinking upon the concept of a world policy.

Part Two is therefore clearly a formidable undertaking; there are difficulties of all sorts to overcome. I am quite clear that in tackling it I shall not avoid all the numerous traps with which the path is strewn; I have nevertheless felt compelled to try, for these questions must be dealt with–however imperfectly–and discussed, since upon them to a large extent depends whether we understand the events in which we are involved and are therefore masters of our future.

Four

Military Consequences of Deterrence

There must obviously be a number of important ways in which knowledge of the laws of deterrence can be applied in practice. We must therefore now come down from the abstract plane on which the analysis of deterrence was necessarily made, and try to see what may be the military consequences of deterrence, first on our ideas about war and in particular about the types of war which may occur, and secondly on the general direction in which our military preparations should be orientated so that they may fit the facts of the new situation.

1 FORMS OF CONFLICT IN THE NUCLEAR AGE

So far in our study of deterrence, we have been concerned with methods of preventing a conflict. A somewhat hazy picture has gradually emerged, rather like the outline of a sketch, and this we must now fill in: what forms of conflict are still possible and what will their characteristics be?

The two questions are comparatively simple, but unfortunately the answers to them are inevitably pretty complicated. In fact deterrence may induce people to give up something, persuade them to avoid something but only exceptionally can it really compel them not to do something. As a result we shall be faced by a whole gamut of forms of conflict none of which has become entirely *impossible* but the likelihood of which will decrease as deterrence becomes more complete.

107

TWO CATEGORIES OF FORMS OF WARFARE

Over-simplifying somewhat, there are two broad categories:

(1) The category directly subject to nuclear deterrence because of the serious risks involved. These are the *types of conflict for which preparation is made in order to make quite sure that they never take place.* Preparation for them is one of the important facets of deterrence but their use is highly improbable.

(2) The category of conflict which may well not give rise to nuclear hazards. This is the *type of conflict for which provision is made in order that it may be employed if necessary.* It is, of course, also subject to deterrence but it may be necessary to have recourse to it in certain circumstances.

At first sight this may seem a somewhat surprising classification; its great advantage, however, is that it sets out and differentiates between those forms of conflict the essential purpose of which is to deter, and those which bear some relation to actual operational possibilities or intentions.

Practicable forms of warfare

We will deal first with Category No. 2, the forms of warfare held to be practicable. (It will be found that they have all been employed since the advent of nuclear weapons.)

The spectrum of this form of warfare is fairly wide but it can be divided into four general types on an ascending scale of military intensity:

1 *Cold war not including guerilla warfare,* using in other words solely politico-diplomatic methods. Here again there are two subdivisions:

Cold war without use of a fifth column (in other words using solely external pressures);

Cold war including use of a fifth column to seize power (combination of external and internal pressures);

There are plenty of examples: Berlin, Latin America, the Congo, Middle East, etc.

2 *Cold war including guerilla warfare*, which we know only too well (Algeria, Vietnam, Angola, Cuba first phase, etc.).

3 *Semi-hot war*, including in addition to the various actions set out above, limited use of conventional military forces as a back-up (Israel, Cuba second phase, Laos, Yemen, etc.).

4 *Limited conventional war*, in which conventional military action takes over from politico-diplomatic methods; action in this category is frequently violent, sometimes protracted but invariably kept within well defined limits, generally by tacit agreement. This was the case in the final phase of the Indo-China campaign, in Korea, Matsu and Quemoy, the Suez-Sinai Campaign, the Sino-Indian conflict and the Bizerta incident.

All these types of conflict have been employed as a normal method during the nuclear age but they have been used only in marginal zones where the nuclear deterrent did not operate. None of them involved use of nuclear weapons.

Improbable forms of warfare

Turning now to the forms of conflict for which preparations are made in order to prevent them happening, we have nothing to go on but hypotheses; there are no instances to confirm them.

Here again the spectrum is very wide and very varied. Most people divide it into two categories: general war and local war.

1 The picture of *general war* has been that of a violent conflict comparable in extent to the two world wars and involving simultaneous use of conventional, nuclear and thermo-nuclear resources. The concept has been of a repetition of 1939–45 using new methods. People soon realized, however, that the form such a war might take could well vary considerably, depending upon the general idea behind it. But in the last thirteen years there has been a major evolution of ideas.

(a) Initially a general war was envisaged as the 'spasm', in other words reaching maximum intensity at the outset. This was a logical concept so long as the problem was to protect oneself against being destroyed by the enemy by crushing him at the earliest possible moment: based on the techniques of air strategy, a unique colossal destructive machine was evolved. Logically this machine should have been used to carry out the surprise attack which was the cause of so much fear but the threat of which was morally impossible. Two hypotheses therefore gained currency: surprise attack by the enemy to which our own action was merely a riposte, or an enemy attack after an alert, in which case our riposte would be more certain and might even be preceded by a 'pre-emptive' attack on our part. As an extreme case, the possibility of preventive attack was discussed.

(b) Very soon, however, the threat of destruction hanging over European and American cities as a result of the existence of Soviet nuclear weapons, threw doubt upon the possibility of using this enormous steam-hammer to solve relatively minor problems. Moreover it was not good enough simply to have one launching plan and so, for want of flexibility, be forced needlessly to destroy a satellite who might declare himself neutral at the last moment. Gradually, therefore, it was realized that two possibilities must be kept open; the first was that of the *delayed spasm riposte*[1] to ensure that if minor incidents occurred, a strike would only be launched with our eyes open and after a test period of conventional warfare; the second was that of *controlled general war*, making it possible to exempt this or that area as required.

(c) When, however, thought was given to possible enemy action, it was realized that he might behave in very different ways: either he could destroy the whole or a part of the population of Europe as he might feel inclined, or alternatively, he might wish to preserve the resources of Europe in order to use them himself. In the first case he would make large-scale use of thermo-nuclear weapons; in the second case he would make *selective use of nuclear weapons* in order to gain a quick local victory and invade Europe, thereby covering himself against an American riposte. On our side, for different reasons, we were led equally to envisage selective use of nuclear weapons, primarily to reduce destruction on allied territory and possibly in the satellite countries to a minimum.

(d) Finally, as the dangers and absurdities of such a form of

[1] Termed 'the pause' by General Norstad.

conflict became clearer, the idea of *progressive general war* was produced, meaning that efforts would be made to keep the use of force at the lowest possible level. On the assumption that the enemy would open hostilities at a low level of intensity (we had travelled a long way from the surprise spasm attack!), the idea was that we should riposte at this level or at the level immediately above, in an attempt to solve the conflict by bargaining and compromise if necessary. If this did not succeed, one side or the other would 'escalate' on to the next level up. Movement up the ladder would therefore take place rung by rung, each step being invariably controlled so as to avoid spontaneous escalation. We have already dealt with this ladder when studying deterrence; its rungs are limited conventional war, use of tactical nuclear weapons, use of strategic nuclear weapons ranging from warning shots to limited counter-force action, thence to general counter-force action and finally to limited counter-city action as a demonstration.

2 *Violent local war*. The general intention being to keep the war limited, it soon became clear that one of the easiest and most effective methods was geographic limitation, used with such remarkable effect in Korea. So, in addition to the 'general war' ladder, there emerged a comparable ladder for violent local wars, christened by the Americans 'theatre wars'. Instead of letting loose the ultimate riposte in the case of every local conflict – the strategy of the 1950's – we arrived at the more or less open admission that no one wanted to extend the conflict but, on the contrary, hoped to deal with it locally. This led to a concept of local wars which, within a restricted geographical area, could have all the gradations we have seen in the case of general war (spasm, delayed, controlled, progressive); they might involve use either of conventional weapons only or of tactical nuclear weapons or strategic nuclear weapons or thermo-nuclear weapons, the last two cases being on the face of it difficult to differentiate from general war.

People in Europe got very excited about this concept of 'theatre wars', particularly when viewed in connection with that of the 'sanctuaries'; they feared that Europe might become a theatre of war while the USSR and United States would be sanctuaries. What people did not realize was that this was no theory of war as such, but merely an additional rung on the escalation ladder and that from the moment it was accepted that the 'spasm' forms of warfare were impossible, there had necessarily to be a number of rungs on the ladder.

But if, in fact, a major conflict in Europe could be kept limited even temporarily—which seems doubtful—what would be its limits? What would be the European Yalu—the Rhine and the Dnieper, the Channel and the Volga, the Atlantic and the Urals? What would happen in the case of Soviet bases situated outside these limits? All these are questions to which there can be no certainty of reply, but as we shall see in a moment, the various possible answers to them may lead to a fundamental change in the whole basis of air warfare.

In any case it must be remembered that the whole concept of violent, but geographically limited, war is based upon the existence of more or less permanent sanctuaries and this would have important implications on logistics and on naval and air operations.

General war and violent local war are therefore in fact no more than different stages in the process of escalation and, since both would be nuclear, our feet would be well on the ladder. For this reason these types of war, though falling outside the limits of nuclear deterrence, are equally improbable since they are quite definitely too dangerous. The only purpose in preparing for this type of war is to ensure that it becomes impossible.

Requirement for an intermediate form of warfare; 'sublimited' nuclear war

If there were no form of nuclear warfare thought to be practicable, the credibility of the nuclear deterrent would fall to zero. To preserve this credibility there must be at least one type of minor nuclear warfare capable of acting as the first step in the escalation process, or at least of causing people to fear that escalation might take place. This opens up the whole problem of first strike credibility discussed at length in connection with deterrence.

We have before us a spectrum as wide as it is varied, ranging from the bottom to the top level of violence; within it are two major sub-divisions, 'non-nuclear practicable wars' and 'highly improbable nuclear wars'; this means that we must devise a type of warfare which can form the connecting link between the two main categories. It must be both practicable – *in extremis* – and nuclear.

This intermediate form of warfare would seem to be '*sublimited*' *nuclear war*; in other words, a war involving the possible but very restricted use of nuclear weapons. How can any nuclear war be 'sublimited'? There are two schools of thought, a fact which shows how conjectural the whole concept is. Some people, Herman Kahn for instance, conceive it merely as a series of strategic warning shots purely psychological in purpose (bombs into the tundra or on Kamchatka for instance). Others such as Kissinger, on the other hand, see these warning shots being directed on to tactical targets (to destroy an invading force or intervene in a defensive battle for instance). In any event the idea would be to use only a very small number of weapons, as opposed to NATO's tactical nuclear concept of recent years envisaging all-out employment of short-range weapons.

Is this concept realistic? No one can say. It is certain, however, that it is the only method of preparing for a demonstration of our determination to embark on escalation with the object of avoiding this type of conflict. It must therefore be considered to be feasible and we must be visibly prepared to use it if we wish first to maintain the deterrent value of the nuclear system, and secondly to retain the ability to reinforce our conventional defensive capacity on a considerable scale. Personally I incline towards the Kissinger theory.

Indisputably, however, this connecting link is a 'must', not of course because we wish to use it but in order to deter, in other words in order to extend the stabilizing effect of the nuclear threat on to the conventional level.

THE VARIOUS OPERATIONAL FORMS

It is not enough, however, simply to differentiate between these various types of war; if these theories are to be translated into possible plans and appropriate combat methods, we must look into their effects on tactics.

It then becomes apparent that the classification above, essential on the total strategy level, no longer fits when we come down to military strategy, still less when dealing with land, air and naval strategy. As an example, the practicable types of warfare, those involving conventional forces, appear to differ considerably when looked at from the viewpoint of total strategy, but in the context of military strategy they are somewhat similar. On the other hand the improbable types of warfare, those involving the use of nuclear weapons, when considered on the military strategy level, are completely different things. To draw the operational conclusions, therefore, we must make a fresh classification based upon the military factors.

Main operational factors

In the search for the operational consequences, our starting point must be the *operational factors*; the main factors are: the intensity of nuclear fire power, the relative capabilities of air forces, navies and armies respectively, the existence or non-existence of geographical limits to the conflict, the capacity or incapacity to keep up a prolonged effort, etc.

1 *Nuclear fire power*. The intensity of nuclear fire power is the prime variable factor:

(a) *All-out* use of the resources available today would make war indistinguishable from the nuclear exchange. In the areas affected the only operations would be survival operations; the situation would be equivalent to an Agadir or Skoplje earthquake multiplied several thousand times. Casualties would be in hundreds of millions. In the literal sense of the word this is an unthinkable cataclysm.

In this situation military forces, if still in existence, could do no more than take part in rescue operations. But in fact there would be no airfields and therefore no aircraft; radio communications would be jammed, all ports would be destroyed and contaminated, cities would be immense charnel houses full of dead and dying; the air would be poisoned by atomic fall-out; life would take refuge underground; there would be no more logistics and no more armed forces. Both sides would be in a similar position.

(b) For this reason people have been forced to envisage only the 'selective' use of nuclear weapons on the lines dealt with above: destruction would be limited to that necessary either to crack the enemy's morale by the symbolic destruction of one or two major cities (on the Hiroshima or Rotterdam model) or to protect oneself against enemy nuclear action (nuclear counter-force action) or to ensure and accelerate a local land or naval victory.

There are therefore already three starting points for this concept; it can be further broken down into numerous subdivisions. The fact is that, except in a simple case of terror attack and in spite of the very large number of nuclear weapons available, there is every chance that in this 'selective' procedure the number of targets will be greater than the number of weapons. Targets must therefore be placed in an order of urgency and, depending on the priorities selected, the operational consequences will be very different.

If the effort is to be directed against the enemy armed forces, are we to concentrate on the destruction of the most modern and the most highly protected weapons (submarines, concrete emplacements), very expensive to destroy, or on equipment such as airfields and radar, already obsolete but giving a better quantitative return? At sea are we to try to destroy submarines, fleets or bases? On land are we to attack the combat echelon and if so in which areas, or shall we try to paralyse the logistic system? Whatever solution is adopted will obviously produce very different operational consequences.

This extreme complication has given rise to the conviction that selective nuclear war can only be conducted with a very highly developed command and control system able to survive an enemy attack. The cost of systems of this nature is at the moment prohibitive for second-rank powers, a fact used to argue the impossibility of having more than one system and so of being able to employ independent nuclear forces profitably.

(c) Nuclear fire power may also be employed *sparingly* with the psychological object of demonstrating determination to resist and acceptance of the risk of escalation. Very limited use of nuclear weapons may produce important operational results if judiciously employed, in other words if used at a decisive time and place. The possibility of such use will force both sides to take more or less permanent anti-nuclear security precautions (dispersion, digging in, etc.).

(d) Finally, *nuclear fire power may not be employed at all*—the most likely case. But, as we have just seen, the nuclear threat remains. This is not to say that conventional war cannot be envisaged at all without continuous anti-nuclear precautions but it does mean that one must have continuously in mind the possibility that the enemy may use a small number of nuclear weapons at a critical moment. For instance a few nuclear weapons used against the landing at Port Said would have turned the operation into a disaster and there would have been no reaction from world opinion. It is for this reason that the 'sublimited' nuclear war category has a foot both in the practicable and improbable camps, and it is for this reason that it is the least improbable type of nuclear war. The fact that it is possible means that we must at all times hold a riposte ready in order to deter the enemy, also that we must never be caught too concentrated in order to avoid presenting the enemy with over-inviting targets offering decisive results to limited nuclear action.

2 *Geographical limits.* If there are geographical limitations, however precarious, they may play an equally important role. If there are such limits, as in Korea, the struggle conducted within them can be supported and fed from without by bases and forces which cannot be attacked. The most important result is that any position of superiority achieved by one side can always be reversed by reinforcements brought in at any time. Superiority can only be temporary. Nuclear or air mastery cannot be achieved. Now this form of geographically limited war is just as applicable to nuclear conflicts as it is to the conventional conflicts we have found to be

practicable. Mentally, therefore, we must be prepared for this possibility, however much it may differ from our traditional naval and air concepts.

3 *Duration.* The duration of the struggle and the capacity to sustain conflict, however long it may be, is a factor frequently disregarded: because the initial concept was of a nuclear 'spasm' war, we have got the idea that war can only be short. It is of course true that the shorter the war the better, but this may well not be the view of the weaker party whose only hope of victory may lie in a long-drawn-out struggle. It should be noted, moreover, that the majority of post-war conflicts have been protracted, the weaker side seeking a decision by playing upon the weariness of his opponent, a highly important facet of psychological strategy. Even in the improbable category there is only one type of war which would undoubtedly be short, the completely improbable hypothesis of the nuclear 'spasm' war.

Capacity to sustain a long war is therefore an essential, even if only for deterrent purposes. But this capacity postulates a military system very different from that designed for a short war: the effort demanded from the country and the armed forces must not be too great; there must be a long-term logistic system and a highly flexible, echelonned mobilization system. These requirements have frequently been lost sight of in recent years.

Operational consequences

From these main operational factors it is possible to deduce the salient characteristics of the nuclear, air, naval and land aspects of the various types of warfare.

1 *In the nuclear field*, deterrence means that we must be prepared for operations at three foreseeable levels of intensity.

(a) It is clearly necessary to be ready with a '*spasm*' *strike* and to let it be known that we are thus prepared. This is the essential minimum to give such an attack credibility and therefore the desired deterrent effect. To ensure that the threat of a 'spasm' attack is valid under all circumstances, the striking force must have a high survival capability.[1] In the present stage of technical development the submarine is the only weapon possessing this essential quality.

(b) But this 'spasm' use of nuclear weapons must not be the only one of which we are capable; we must be able to play tunes on the strategic use of these weapons ranging from the most violent counter-city action down to demonstrations of a purely psychological nature or the destruction of enemy forces and intervention in the land-air battle. It is therefore essential that the command system and signals network should be such as to ensure *controlled use* of nuclear weapons. This is a vast problem when it is remembered that the command system must be capable of functioning on the second strike, in other words after the devastation caused by an enemy's first strike.

Such a system is already an essential for the major nuclear powers, the United States and the USSR, who are carrying the whole weight of the world nuclear balance. It does not apply in the same way to the second-rank nuclear powers like Great Britain and France, who are concerned in the nuclear game primarily only from the deterrence point of view; in their case a riposte following a major enemy first strike is a highly unlikely contingency. The technical difficulties and high cost of a fully developed system need not therefore lead us to reject a more makeshift type of system which would clearly not survive a first enemy strike; such a system is necessary at all times to guarantee that the game of deterrence can be played with the necessary flexibility.

(c) Finally we must have a system of *tactical nuclear weapons*. Here again, however, we must be on our guard against extremist concepts: the massive employment of tactical nuclear weapons, until recently the SHAPE doctrine, is analogous to and as improbable as the 'spasm' use of strategic weapons. The least improbable use of nuclear weapons is limited intervention in the land-air or naval-air conventional battle at a decisive time and place to ensure a quick local victory or prevent a rapid local

---

[1] This somewhat general conclusion needs qualification in the case of a 'third party' covered by a major ally (see Chapter Three above).

defeat. Practical study and the outcome thereof, development of the most suitable weapons system, should be concentrated upon this type of employment and the corresponding counters to it.

2 *In air warfare*, using the term in its strict sense of the word (and the same applies to naval and land warfare), there would seem to be four operational systems corresponding to the four degrees of intensity of use of nuclear weapons ranging from the 'spasm' to refusal to use them at all. As already explained, the most probable are the two bottom levels where the smallest degree of force is used. These are therefore the most important.

(a) Assuming nuclear weapons were not employed, the air battle would have certain interesting characteristics. Since the last war the aim of the air battle has been held to be air mastery. From 1943 onwards, however, this was the result (and on the Allied side only) of considerable numerical superiority. With the comparatively small numbers available in peace-time, adequate destructive capacity could only be maintained by the use of nuclear weapons. If, therefore, nuclear weapons are not used, the mutual attrition of the opposing air forces will be slow. The effect of anti-aircraft defences based on ground-to-air missiles will equally be small. In short, it seems likely that the air battle will be indecisive—apart from cases in which there is great disparity in numbers and morale between the two sides as at Suez—and will result in situations of local and more or less temporary air superiority, the major role being played by fighters equipped with air-to-air missiles. On the other hand, the possible employment by the defence of ground-to-air missiles with nuclear warheads would almost inevitably preclude the use of the major bomber formations of the last war.

The air battle would be even more indecisive if the conflict was geographically limited and a sizeable proportion of the opposing air forces was outside the theatre of operations.

There would also be a considerable change in the nature of air support available for the land battle; numbers being smaller, the air battle being more prolonged and the requirements for air cover presumably taking priority, only a small number of aircraft would remain available for ground support; the large-scale 1945 influence of air power on land operations would undoubtedly be considerably reduced.

(b) These conclusions are applicable only to the conventional or 'sublimited' form of air warfare; they must be re-thought completely in the case of *controlled nuclear warfare*, as soon as this reaches a level of violence sufficient to make general counterforce action possible.

In this event, there are several possibilities:

If one side gains air mastery quickly, the resulting superiority will make it possible for him to intervene on a large scale in the land-air battle. The air aspect will become overriding.

If the mutual attrition on both sides is high, the residual air forces will not be able to play any very great role.

If mutual attrition affects only the more vulnerable of the two air forces, that which is tied to the conventional airfields, the remaining STOL or VTOL aircraft would engage in a second air battle and the decision would to a great extent depend upon the relative performance – even if low – of these aircraft.

(c) Finally in the event of '*spasm*' *nuclear warfare*, air warfare in the strict sense of the word would be almost as futile as land-air warfare: airfields and navigation aids would be destroyed, radio communications would be jammed, atomic fall-out would contaminate emergency landing grounds, etc.

To sum up both the action and the value of air forces will vary fundamentally with each hypothesis. The same applies to the possibility of airborne or air-transported operations. Planning must therefore be extremely flexible and enable us to adapt ourselves to any situation which may eventuate.

3 *In naval-air warfare* changes may be almost equally far-reaching. Apart from the role played by naval forces in the strategic nuclear battle, the object of naval forces is to establish general or local command of the sea by destroying the enemy forces. Previously this was done by gunfire, then in 1939–45 by air forces, usually carrier borne; the tendency now is to use missiles. The development of the submarine, however, has given a new dimension to naval warfare and necessitated the use of a lighter type of vessel, both for submarine chasing and convoy protection.

(a) *If the war remains conventional* the air aspect still has all its importance and the aircraft carrier remains an essential feature. On the other hand, without nuclear depth charges the anti-submarine war may be less effective. It will be more difficult to ensure safety of the sea routes. The struggle for command of the sea would be fought out primarily between aircraft and submarines.

(b) In this situation a few *nuclear weapons* may play a highly important role: the destruction of two or three aircraft carriers or a few nuclear submarines might give one side or the other an appreciable tactical or political advantage. Moreover, there being no population in sea areas, nuclear explosions are psychologically less dangerous than on land. For this reason, 'sublimited' nuclear warfare would seem to be particularly credible in the naval-air field as providing a method of political pressure with a minimum of risk.

(c) In controlled but sufficiently intense nuclear warfare, the operational considerations would be very different: bases and ports could easily be put out of action; major surface vessels would be detected and tracked by satellites and so would more than likely be destroyed (in spite of what has been said on this subject in connection with the Multilateral Force proposed by the Americans). The submarine, whether missile carrying or not, would be the decisive factor and the aircraft carrier would lose its usefulness. Surface navigation would become extremely dangerous.

(d) Finally, in *paroxysmal nuclear warfare* the basic role of naval forces would, in the first instance, be to participate in the nuclear battle, using primarily missile-carrying submarines. In the areas attacked, ports would no longer exist.

After the destruction phase and the succeeding pause, the navy, using such vessels as remained, would have to take part in supplying the devastated areas from other regions still intact.

4 *In land-air warfare*, in addition to the variables of nuclear war, there are those peculiar to land warfare; the number of hypotheses is therefore even greater.

The reason is that land operations in themselves may differ

considerably in accordance with the relationship between tactical and strategic mobility and between defensive and offensive capacity. Depending on the relative importance of these tactical factors, operations may vary from a war of movement to position warfare, as happened between 1914 and 1945.[1] In order therefore to try and forecast the form which land operations might take, an estimate must be made of the influence exerted upon these tactical factors by the nuclear and air factors and by the factors stemming from the equipment available to the land forces.

(a) *In conventional warfare* we have dealt with the probable characteristics of the air factor and seen that its influence upon land operations will undoubtedly be limited. At this point, however, two most important land factors come into play: in the first place land forces are now fully mechanized and the mobility of both sides will therefore be high; secondly, the size of land forces will be very small compared to the area of the theatre of operations. Conventional warfare will therefore be a highly decisive war of movement characterized by action on widely separated axes.

The availability of auxiliary, satellite or territorial militia forces would make it possible to re-establish a certain degree of continuity in the occupation, or rather surveillance, of ground and enable widespread guerilla action to be undertaken against enemy penetration. Large-scale development of anti-tank resources would also lead to greater operational stability. If, however, the air situation made it possible for one side to carry out air-transported operations, that side might well achieve decisive operational superiority in the theatre concerned.

(b) This being the general form of operations, the use of a *small number of tactical nuclear weapons* might serve to break up any too threatening enemy offensive or conversely deal rapidly with any local enemy defences holding up a decision. 'Sublimited' nuclear action might therefore be able to delay or accelerate a decision, as the case may be, and this, from the total strategy point of view, might be vital.

In any case the threat of nuclear action must inevitably have

---

[1] See *Introduction to Strategy*, Chapter II, 'Traditional Military Strategy'.

some stabilizing effect, since the aggressor will be forced to avoid any major offensive concentration over any length of time. Equally the defence cannot be based on a heavily manned linear system. The layout must be in depth, adequately echelonned, even dispersed.

(c) *If the war takes the form of intense controlled nuclear warfare* very wide dispersion on land becomes essential. Attention would then focus upon the mobility of which land forces might still be capable – and so to some extent therefore upon their logistics.

The side having air superiority, and therefore having his rear areas protected and being able to use air-transported operations, would be able to gain maximum advantage from his mobility. The other side would be lost, as was France in 1940.

If, on the other hand, the air factor is of reduced importance owing to the mutual attrition of the opposing air forces, STOL or VTOL transport aircraft may play a decisive role. If, however, nuclear fire power is used both intensively and continuously, the offensive capacity of land forces and the possibility of supplying them will be much reduced; land operations may then tend towards a sort of dispersed stabilization with guerilla forces acting as the outposts and probably operating also in the interior of the areas concerned.

(d) Finally, in *'spasm' nuclear warfare*, land forces can do no more than disperse, dig in and take part as best they can in civil defence, in other words in rescue operations for which their organization and signal facilities suit them. They may be able to play a vital role in the cataclysm, always provided that preparations for that role have been made.

These are the conclusions which seem to me to result from an objective study. I wish they could have been simpler. I hope that, nevertheless, they will help to clear the mind.

They should do so if we keep before us two facts: first, the basic distinction which must be drawn today between the practicable types of warfare; secondly, the infinite variety of situations with which we may be faced if, in spite of deterrence, fate decrees that we must once more play our part in some major conflict.

2 THE MILITARY SYSTEM OF THE NUCLEAR AGE

GENERAL OUTLINE OF THE PROBLEM

Complexity

The non-expert reader may justifiably be surprised at the complexity of the problem and the variety of the hypotheses deduced from even a cursory analysis of the military prospects stemming from nuclear deterrence. This complexity, moreover, explains the confusion and woolliness characteristic of this subject; our military arrangements consequently appear conjectural and uncertain, sometimes even mythical. This is serious, for on this subject confidence is absolutely essential. As a result, the military are intellectually in disarray, some taking refuge in scepticism, others in refusal to think.

Uncertainty

Added to this uncertainty of doctrine is the uncertainty resulting from the facts that the world is in a state of evolution, governments both friendly and enemy change frequently, ideas are being transformed and situations turned upside down with frightening rapidity.

We are presumed to know about all this but we forget it just the same. Think back to 1939 and compare the world situation of twenty-five years ago with that of today; then try to picture the differences of the same sort in the hypothetical situations of 1989, twenty-five years ahead. Where will Europe, France and NATO be then? What will be the relations between the United States and the USSR and between the USSR and China? What will be the position of Africa, the Middle East and Latin America?

Up to now man has not proved very adept at looking into the future. Who, prior to 1940, would have forecast that there would be Germans in Biarritz, landings in Normandy and Southern France, the scuttling of our fleet in Toulon, Japanese in Singapore, Rommel in Egypt, etc.? When I took part in laying out the Mareth Line in

Southern Tunisia in 1933, who would have said that it would be occupied by the Germans and taken by the British? When the Colonial Exhibition took place in Vincennes in 1931, who would have said that we were on the eve of decolonization?

Necessity for an adaptable system

Changing times and an unpredictable future present the architect of a defence system with a problem of extreme difficulty.

The difficulty is increased by the fact that each era has its established truth learnedly propounded by the prophets and leaders of the time but only very seldom confirmed by the facts. Surprise resulting from the unforeseen is the rule even for an aggressor, who can choose his moment and his methods. The result is that any military system designed completely in accordance with the forecasts and to meet solely the situation envisaged by those forecasts, runs a grave risk of being disproved by the course of events. We must therefore be on our guard against solutions conforming too closely to the hypotheses and theories in fashion at the moment. They could be very dangerous. A military system must not be a tailor-made suit but an adjustable garment which any sized man can wear.

All this means that defence must be looked at, not as a rigid structure, but as a basis worked out in broad terms and so manipulated that it can accept a constant process of adaptation without its foundations being affected. To paraphrase Poincaré's remark about peace, national defence can be nothing other than a 'continuous creation' based upon an infrastructure the main qualities of which must be adaptability and polyvalence.

Between 1939 and 1963, France has been through no less than thirteen major military changes: the 1939 armed forces, mobilization, the armistice army, the Free French forces, the army of Africa, the Italian Expeditionary Corps, the French Forces of the Interior, the First French Army, the transition army, the French forces of the Far East, of Germany, of NATO, the armed forces in Algeria, the force de frappe, mobile reserve and so on and so forth . . .

No hypothesis should be eliminated

In spite of this continual process of change, we have each time tried to solve our problem by a system based upon an *a priori* choice of a single solution held at the time to be overriding. In the old days it was the continuous front and the power of the defensive; today it is the nuclear weapon.

The great error is that each school of thought always tries to put forward its conclusion as the only true solution. Just as with total strategy, people have not realized that it is impossible to produce a single simple answer to a complicated fluid problem. All the hypotheses are there, some more probable than others, but no one can be sure that any one of them will tell us what will actually occur to the exclusion of all the others. Moreover, people have often not grasped the distinction I have emphasized here between preparations intended to deter and those concerned with military action which might actually be carried out.

I believe that the truth lies in accepting the fact that a multiplicity of solutions is possible. The present situation is the antithesis of that prior to 1939 when the existence of a predetermined enemy and of a single operational doctrine (which proved to be a wrong one) gave rise to a deadening sterilizing dogmatism. Dogmatism in any form has now become impossible: there can be no more comforting but ossifying regulations: today we are forced to be *ready to adapt ourselves* practically instantaneously to the most varied and perhaps least foreseeable situations.

To do this we must work our imagination hard, trying to forecast possible situations in order not to be taken too much by surprise and above all in order to foresee the measures necessary to meet these various situations. We must also strive for flexibility of mind and capacity for decision. Finally, we must have an organization based upon the necessity for rapid adaptation. All this involves great changes in some of our traditional ideas.

Choice of the constant factors on which to base an organization

In spite, however, of this all-pervading and inevitable uncertainty, we have got to work out the essential foundations upon which the overall organization of the forces, choice of equipment and training can be based. In this shifting sand we have got to find fixed points to which to anchor our day-to-day arrangements.

First among these constant factors must come the great permanent tasks of the armed forces:

To prevent war: the strategy of deterrence;

To support national policy: indirect strategy;

To win the war: war strategy.

1 *Deterrence* has been studied in great detail in this book. The types of resources required for it have been stated: a strategic nuclear force, conventional forces and tactical nuclear weapons. All three are necessary because of the variable nature of nuclear deterrence.

In so far as deterrence is concerned it may well be asked how large the 'necessary' forces should be. This is a highly complex question to which there is only one simple answer: one does the best one can. The dividend one can expect from them naturally depends on what one has been able to put in. If second strike destructive capability is of the order of 50 per cent or more of enemy resources, deterrence can be absolute, in other words both offensive and defensive, always provided that the first strike is 'credible'. If destructive capability is small but nevertheless significant (5 to 15 per cent of enemy resources), one will have a *defensive* deterrent capability only. In this event and if one is in the position of a third party, it will not be essential to have a high survival capability for, as we have seen, the hypothesis of preventive attack by the enemy is highly improbable. If destructive capability is very small, though still not zero, deterrent effect will be highly precarious if not non-existent. Nevertheless, even under present conditions and with future developments in prospect, any deterrent capability, however small, may have considerable political consequences.

Turning now to the deterrent exerted by conventional forces complementing that of the nuclear deterrent, it is clear that here again one does the best one can – and the best will be that much smaller as the effort devoted to the nuclear field becomes greater (the Russians have had to reduce their conventional forces by nearly 40 per cent since they have developed their nuclear forces). Moreover, modern conventional equipment is extremely expensive; one is therefore forced to restrict the size of forces to something far smaller than that to which we have become accustomed in previous periods (West Germany without a nuclear force can hardly raise more than twelve divisions; France with a nuclear force has only five or six divisions compared to the thirty peace-time divisions of 1938). Thanks to the Western Alliance, forces of this restricted size are adequate to provide the necessary complement to the nuclear deterrent so long as the latter remains at its present significant level. Should nuclear deterrence tend to cancel itself out, as is always possible, it would be necessary to have larger conventional forces, even if the additional equipment had to be of a less modern type. *Capacity to increase size* of conventional forces is absolutely essential to guard against possible changes in the situation. Various methods, on the face of it practicable and not unduly costly, can be devised to do this. I shall deal with them under the heading of national defence tasks.

2   The contribution to *indirect strategy* made by military forces implies possible use, in addition to the influence of nuclear and military potential, of a *mobile strategic reserve.*

The role this force will play, like the course of events, can generally not be foreseen. (In 1950, for instance, who could have foreseen that we should be in action at Suez or Bizerta?) To be effective, the mobile reserve must have three characteristics:

Availability at all times, so that it can be put into action more or less instantaneously (not after a long preparatory period as in the Suez affair);

Mobility by air and sea: transport aircraft, transport for vehicles, amphibious equipment, helicopters and helicopter carriers, support aircraft and aircraft carriers; all are required for rapid, flexible intervention;

Strength: this will vary in each particular case and depends on that of the enemy. It must be possible to vary the composition of the mobile reserve according to circumstances; the troops may be differently equipped and the units required may vary depending on the task in view.

Finally it is desirable that the force should have bases available within easy range. Since existing bases have become highly precarious in the present day world, aircraft carriers have become essential as mobile bases.

3   The task of military forces *in the event of war* presents at first sight an insoluble problem: deterrence will have failed and one will be faced with forms of warfare previously classified as improbable; the intensity at which the war will be conducted will not be foreseeable; it may range from wholesale nuclear destruction of populations to conventional war on the frontiers with possibly 'sublimited' nuclear incidents. This points up the extreme difficulty of the present situation: the effort required to prepare oneself for all the numerous differing and somewhat improbable hypotheses is out of all proportion. It is for this reason that the only intelligent solution is to concentrate upon deterrence.

Nevertheless the fact that the improbable war remains a possibility, and a possibility carrying with it a risk of the utmost seriousness, compels us to make provision for *minimum* precautionary measures to guard against the extreme but deadly eventuality.

Although the likelihood of a full-scale nuclear conflict is small, we cannot abandon altogether preparations for civil defence, possible decentralization of government, internal local defence and even more important, measures to ensure continuity of governmental action. This is a question, however, not so much of costly material preparations (shelters and drugs in particular) as of organization and the inculcation of a state of mind capable of withstanding the surprise which leads to catastrophe.

Similarly in the atomic era, the notion of armed invasion of the 1939–45 type seems barely credible. Nevertheless NATO, formed at a time when nuclear deterrence was not yet adequate, was founded upon this concept. Today, therefore, we have the advantage of a collective defence system of considerable defensive value, primarily because it is unlikely ever to have to be used. It is almost certain that, without the use of nuclear weapons, NATO's defensive system is incapable of prolonged resistance to large-scale invasion by conventional forces; this does not mean, however, that our defence is inadequate, for the present level of nuclear deterrence makes it impossible for our opponent to carry out this type of invasion. In the NATO framework, therefore, the possibility of conventional war is very adequately covered, at any rate for the present.

We have seen, however, that nuclear deterrence may reach a state of mutual paralysis. Hypothetical though this case may be, it is still possible and it would necessitate recourse to larger-scale conventional forces. For this reason, first for deterrent purposes and then in case of war, it is essential that we have a military system permitting us to revert to the relatively large-scale numbers considered by some writers definitely obsolete in the nuclear age.

Since we are trying to guard against a possibility only, there is no sense in keeping a large-scale military establishment permanently in existence but we must be able to go over to one quickly and smoothly if necessary. Personally I believe that there can be no satisfactory solution to this problem so long as, for this category of force, we go on clinging to our present military system based on relatively long-term service personnel; the reserves thus produced are no better than collections of individuals formed into *ad hoc* units without cohesion or collective training. A militia system on Swiss army lines with a very short period of active service followed by short call-ups at frequent intervals, puts life into reserve units and makes considerable expansion possible at the lowest possible standing cost. This militia should be organized by areas and possibly by age groups; it would thus be a crucible for local civic spirit—which our army has ceased to be. At the same time it would be an extremely flexible reservoir of manpower, ready to meet those cases in which larger-scale forces were necessary, either for local and civil defence or for participation in the battle, or even to reinforce indirect strategy action.

I know that some people think this a dangerously retrograde idea. I believe that that is a point of view based on conclusions stemming too directly from considerations of the moment: only a short while ago we had to keep 400,000 men in Algeria and who can say what we shall require ten years hence? Great Britain thought that she could cut down her forces and revert to a professional army, but the simultaneous crises of Cyprus, Zanzibar and Malaysia produced requirements far greater than she could cope with and forced her into a dangerous internationalization of the Cyprus affair. In Europe itself, if there were grave social upheavals in the territory of one of our neighbours, Spain or Italy for instance, we might be faced with a large-scale frontier protection problem.

Finally, there is the question of internal security at home. I approach this problem with some hesitation for I am personally averse to considering the armed forces as an instrument for maintenance of law and order, an idea much in fashion a few years ago: that is the job of the police forces, available in France in large numbers; but it is clear that the police cannot guard everything and were there to be conflicts or disturbances, considerable forces would be required for security, civil defence, air defence and defence against possible parachute landings.

All these reasons add up to a good case for the organization in France of a real militia alongside our permanent fighting forces. This would solve many problems simultaneously: in the first place it would form a more economical military cadre than that we at present possess and one more capable of providing for all the possible requirements to which the various hypotheses may give rise; secondly, it would make possible a considerable reduction in the length of military service in this category of unit and that at a moment when, owing to the growth of population, there is a dangerous tendency to abandon the principle that every Frenchman should bear arms in defence of his country;[1] finally, it would renew the local links between people and the armed forces which at present have vanished completely.

In my view a militia system is an essential element of any military system in the nuclear age because it alone can most easily and most cheaply be adapted to infinitely varying unforeseen circumstances. We should then have a three-tier military structure:

For nuclear deterrence, a nuclear force;

[1] The result of a selective service scheme would be to produce a category of Frenchmen exempt from military service.

For complementary deterrence, frontier protection and intervention elsewhere, conventional armed forces limited in size but available at all times;

For defence in all its forms, a national militia.

Choice of the basic option

But it is not enough simply to set out the overall structure. We must also decide upon the types of force we wish to produce and therefore upon their equipment and training.

There can be no question of preparing for one situation only – even if it appears to be the most likely; the only logical aim is to prepare to adapt oneself to meet the unknown; we are therefore drawn straightaway to a system capable of dealing with the two extreme types of warfare, holding in reserve what is necessary to guard against the unforeseen:

(a) For deterrence purposes, *we must make open preparations for 'spasm' nuclear warfare* but we must be able to control it and to manipulate its initiation. We must be quite clear that the only object of the national or NATO exercises on this theme is to check and improve the efficiency of deterrence. They do not produce a picture of the war we reckon to wage but of that we wish to prevent.

(b) We must be ready to conduct mobile conventional warfare in a more or less limited area and over a more or less prolonged period of time, but taking into account always the possibility of rounding it off by *'sublimited' nuclear action* and by guerilla warfare. Our equipment and unit training must be such that we can conduct both these forms of warfare; detailed instructions on how to do so should be issued to the lower levels. For the intermediate and higher levels, on the other hand, there should be frequent two-sided exercises without troops to prepare them mentally for the intermediate forms of warfare.

By starting from the two extremes, it will always be possible to adjust oneself to the concrete situations which may arise.

(c) *Finally we must be ready to adapt ourselves to unforeseen situations* differing completely from anything we had imagined; this necessitates an economical system of organization capable of coping with the maximum number of possible situations and providing a flexible and efficient mechanism both for a rapid increase in numbers by mobilization and for progressive expansion as circumstances may demand. This will be the job of the national militia.

CONCLUSIONS

To deal at the correct level with the problem of the military consequences of deterrence has entailed taking the reader into a field of more specialized discussion than that of the other chapters.

It may serve to give him an idea of the complexity of present-day military problems.

I have tried to keep to the guiding principle; my primary object has been to show that the uncertainty which has always been the lot of the strategist, is greater today than it has ever been; there can therefore be no simple, radical solution.

More than ever before the measures we take must be valid for many differing situations; we must at all times be on the watch, ready to manœuvre and adapt ourselves to circumstances.

3 OVERALL CONCLUSIONS ON THE MILITARY CONSEQUENCES OF DETERRENCE

In this quick run over the military problem of the nuclear age, I have tried to bring out the most characteristic aspects.

(1) First there is the *uncertainty* of the form which any conflict low in the scale of probability might take. This uncertainty is of course no new factor but it is greater than it has ever been, so much so that today we are compelled to take account of it, and that makes any forecast terribly complicated.

Fortunately there are also certain firm *fixed points*: the unchanging tasks of the armed forces and the clear necessity of preparing for the two extreme forms of warfare, paroxysmal nuclear war and mobile conventional war, so being in a position to adapt ourselves to any situation falling between the two.

This leads to a three-tier *military structure*: a nuclear deterrent force, conventional armed forces (including tactical nuclear weapons), a national militia.

(2) *The absolute primacy of deterrence*, war in its most violent form having now become impracticable and far too dangerous to be allowed to occur in the more sensitive areas of the globe. Military forces must therefore be designed and used primarily for the purpose of deterrence.

A deterrent purpose may be traditional (to the Swiss Army, for instance) but to our military men of today, brought up through twenty years of continuous war, it has not much glamour attached. Moreover, does not the advent of the nuclear weapon mark the opening of a new era from which war would be banished? Finally, taking these two ideas together, people naturally wonder whether service in the armed forces is not a somewhat anachronistic form of activity. The question merits an answer, for, more or less implicitly, it is at the root of the attitude adopted by many of my countrymen to the profession of arms; it also exerts a direct influence upon the recruitment of our professional cadre and even upon the confidence they must have in the usefulness of their day-to-day business.

After the great upheaval of 1939–45, the military and ideological confrontation between East and West, combined with the decolonization fever which in the course of a few years laid Europe's world empire in ruins, gave to the profession of arms a high priority both in 'defence' of Europe and for the unending succession of colonial wars. Today, the '*Tiers Monde*' (third world) has gained full independence almost everywhere and, as a result of the nuclear weapon, the contest between Russia and the United States is tending towards equilibrium; undoubtedly, therefore, we are entering calmer waters, at least for the immediate future. But can we say that we are sure of remaining at peace?

As between Russia and the United States, the logic of nuclear deterrence, illustrated by the Cuba crisis, undoubtedly opens up prospects of great stability. As we have seen on several occasions, anxiety over the 'defence' of Europe has lost much of its urgency but that is not because all 'danger' has disappeared: it is because deterrence is operative. The form of the danger has changed: the risk today is not the brutal invasion of the history books; it is one of a slow subtle political slide which may result in major change in the world balance; from this point of view the future of Germany is a vital factor. On the other hand, it would be a great mistake to think that the present deterrent situation will last for ever: it has been subject to constant alteration over the last ten years and there is no reason why it should not continue to be so, with all the changes in whatever direction that may imply. It is for this reason that I have emphasized so strongly the requirement for a military system adaptable to all circumstances. If one day nuclear deterrence were to lose its effectiveness[1] we need not necessarily have 'war' on the twentieth-century model, but we might well be faced with grave danger resulting from manœuvres in the indirect strategy 'mode'; so long as Europe has not arrived at a fair settlement of the problem created by the division of Germany and the subjugation of the satellites, she will not have regained her equilibrium and true European peace will always be precarious.

As far as the '*Tiers Monde*' is concerned, we shall see in the next chapter that the prospects are even more disturbing: the chaos which is the almost invariable successor to colonial domination, is a permanent cause of instability. So far this instability has given rise only to minor or localized conflicts because nuclear deterrence has imposed a high degree of restraint upon military action by the United States and the USSR. Here again evolution in the technicalities of deterrence may lead to large-scale and highly dangerous changes, all the more so since the West in general and France in particular are fairly directly involved in a number of areas. Particularly in the Mediterranean Europe may find herself faced with a most disturbing situation.

Even accepting the fact, however, that nuclear deterrence ought to continue for a long time to come to prevent recourse to force of arms, we must not forget the distant but inexorable problems to which the '*Tiers Monde*' will give rise; when that world has assimilated western techniques and made its great transmutation, Europe will indeed have need of all its strength to survive.

So in the short term as in the long, the task of national defence

---

[1] Quite apart from new technical discoveries, this might happen at any moment as the result of an ill-judged arms control agreement.

appears, as throughout history, to be an essential complement to economic prosperity and cultural progress. The three functions are linked like the limbs of the same body.

The military function remains but its form changes: the advent of mass destruction weapons gives to deterrence a role at present overriding and so opens up an ever wider field of action to indirect strategy with its minor manifestations of violence. We must reckon, however, that the minor forms of violence used by indirect strategy may under certain circumstances become far more violent. Today we have to have more 'technicians' than formerly, but we still have the same need of alert and determined 'gladiators'.

Most important of all, however, is to preserve the defence spirit, our civilization's instinct to survive; history condemns only those peoples who refused to defend themselves. This is the great danger inherent in our material progress and it is the most frequent reason for barbarians taking over from the civilized. If we are to ensure that the third millennium does not take us back to a new Merovingian age, we must know how to keep alive the virtues of determination to act and a spirit of self-sacrifice to an ideal, for which the armed forces have always been the repository. The toughness of their training should be the natural antidote to the easy-going bourgeois way of life which goes with good living.

For this reason, however technical and specialized armed forces may become, they must remain 'national' in the widest sense of the word, in other words they must have their roots deep in the country and be closely bound to it. For this reason, alongside the technicians and the gladiators we now require the soldier-citizen concept produced by a militia. For all these reasons solid national military institutions must be maintained and preserved.

Five

The Strategic Consequences of Deterrence

Working up the scale, we have now reached the final stage of this study. It is now time to tackle the problem of the consequences of the nuclear weapon and of deterrence in general upon world strategy as envisaged today. This is clearly the most difficult phase. The analysis which follows must not be considered as more than an initial outline; its primary object is to show the applicability of the process of strategic reasoning to the present world context.

The arguments I shall be putting forward to some extent clearly overstep the limits of the strategic field in the strict sense of the word, for strategy is only the implementation of a policy. There can be no question of discussing here political problems as such; but the various consequences of any policy must be brought out. I shall be doing so, however, not with any idea of proposing solutions but primarily to provide *examples* of the points which strategy must consider and to highlight the new environment, the new possibilities and the new relationship existing between the various problems. This will, I hope, make clear the type of suggestion which the strategist may have to make to the politician and which it is the duty of the politician to examine; but, at his risk and peril, the politician is unquestionably at liberty to reject these suggestions if they do not conform to his selected political line.

1 PRESENT DAY CHARACTERISTICS OF WORLD STRATEGY

There are two complementary and interdependent aspects to world strategy:

First, the *direct strategy of deterrence*; this is basically nuclear and is moving towards military equilibrium between the great industrial and economic powers; it constitutes an increasingly onerous burden for the most highly developed countries.

Secondly, *indirect strategy*; basically this is political and economic; it may be violent; its intensity depends upon the freedom of action permitted by the neutralizing effect of the military equilibrium. This strategy makes maximum use of the factors of instability, particularly in the '*Tiers Monde*' (Third World).

CONSEQUENCES OF DETERRENCE IN THE DIRECT STRATEGY FIELD

In Part One, we dealt with the various consequences of deterrence. We must now gather up our somewhat scattered conclusions and combine them into an overall picture.

(1) The most important and most obvious consequence is that the major military powers neutralize each other owing to the disproportionate risk with which each faces the other. In the present stage of technical development this neutralizing effect is tending to increase.

(2) The result is that the danger of an East-West thermo-nuclear conflict has become very small, if not nil–the exact opposite of what was thought only a few years ago.

Similarly the danger of a military invasion of Europe by the 'Soviet hordes', which seemed a plausible hypothesis in the Stalinist period, has lost almost all credibility.

(3) These two consequences combine to give our age certain new and peculiar characteristics: in those areas covered by the nuclear deterrent (Berlin or Quemoy, for instance), situations which are politically or strategically absurd, have become so stable as to be almost petrified. In these areas military stability produces almost complete paralysis, however unstable the situation may be politically. Oddly enough, however, this phenomenon is not of general applica-

tion; it stands out in sharp contrast to the almost total instability ruling elsewhere.

(4) There are many reasons for this instability and we shall deal with them in a moment. There is one, however, stemming direct from nuclear strategy. The fact that in certain areas the two major military powers neutralize each other means that in the rest of the world the powers in general, whether strong or weak, have very wide *freedom of action*; but this freedom of action can be exercised only outside the nuclear field and it is less wide for the nuclear powers than for the others.

This freedom of action is somewhat surprising and we have only gradually come to realize that it exists. It is this which has made possible Titoism, Chinese separatism and more recently the independent policy of France. It is being consciously exploited by Castroism and Nasserism, as indeed it was unconsciously by the various revolutionary decolonization movements.

Despite the world's modern armaments therefore, there is now no world policeman, a situation we have not had to face for a long time. Even the small-time agitator can raise almost insoluble international problems (Cyprus for instance) and this makes indirect strategy formidably effective.

(5) But this freedom of action is still only semi-explored. We have not yet really defined the geographical limits within which the deterrent effect of the nuclear weapon operates and, as we have seen, these limits depend to a large extent upon 'credibility'. Credibility is basically a subjective factor to which we must pay careful attention if it is to retain its validity.

Conversely, we do not yet really know to what extent conventional forces have regained their freedom of action. The inhibitions stemming from the fear of nuclear escalation still remain and so any use of force is generally considered highly dangerous. Our basic analysis of the nuclear and conventional levels, however, showed that the former was essentially stable and the latter essentially unstable; it also showed that, unless the two levels are linked (primarily by tactical nuclear weapons), the conventional level may be almost entirely unaffected by nuclear deterrence.

If, therefore, we abandon use of tactical nuclear weapons, we

THE STRATEGIC CONSEQUENCES OF DETERRENCE

must anticipate the recurrence of conventional type military conflict—though temporarily only perhaps—should nuclear deterrence return to a happy instability. The relative importance of conventional forces may thereby be considerably increased.

(6) Another consequence of nuclear deterrence is that mutual danger and the effort entailed in the nuclear arms race creates a sense of solidarity between the nuclear powers. This solidarity has produced a new type of relationship between the Americans and the Russians; it is characterized by a permanent dialogue, open haggling, mutual mistrust and undercover complicity. When the risks to both of them are clearly greater than the issue at stake (e.g. Suez) it might well be that their *de facto* solidarity would be translated into concerted action or even a temporary alliance. The prospect of a world controlled by a *de facto* Russo-American 'condominium' is one of the possible—and menacing—results of nuclear evolution.

Looked at from this point of view, the existence of independent nuclear forces should constitute a guarantee that the interests of the other nuclear powers will not be sacrificed through some agreement between the two super-powers; moreover, if one day, as seems possible, a 'concert of nuclear powers' should emerge, it will be a wider community and the second-rank nuclear powers will not be excluded.

This is a particularly important conclusion.

Moreover, it is clear that the crushing expenditure entailed in the nuclear arms race must make each of the two major opponents want a real truce in order to divert to peaceful purposes the enormous sums now spent entirely unproductively.

Economically and socially there can be no question that a policy of disarmament or reduction of armaments is desirable. The fact remains, however, that from the strategic point of view, any step towards limitation of armaments would be highly dangerous if it increased global instability—it would in fact be false economy. It is essential therefore that any such measures be carefully studied to ensure that they contribute to stability rather than the reverse.

(7) Finally, it must not be forgotten that nuclear deterrence is by nature evolutionary and fluid. Yet it is both the foundation and the scaffolding for the present day structure of peace.

It would therefore be highly dangerous to act as if the neutralization of today were a permanently established fact; it can be upset at any moment by unpredictable technical innovations. Moreover, we must not lose sight for a moment of the essential role which the United States plays in this field for the benefit of us all; if the United States were to lose the edge they have contrived to maintain in the nuclear field, the consequences for all of us would be most serious and our national resources would not suffice to retrieve the situation.

It is therefore our duty to do nothing which might reduce the value of the US global deterrent (just as it is the duty of the United States to put a stop to the wastage of money involved in their narrow policy of 'nuclear secrecy'). This forces us to maintain the Atlantic Alliance; it has perhaps already been our salvation and is the keystone of the deterrence equilibrium in the present day world. It is right, however, that we should try to introduce into the Alliance a control system more in consonance with the situation produced by the revival of Europe and of the European powers. *But the Atlantic Alliance as a strategic entity will be basic to our security for a long time to come.* The modifications to be made to it may have various political repercussions and some of these may lead to decisions apparently to the good. They will not be to the good, however, if they tend to reduce the deterrent influence of the Alliance as a whole. This is the strategic criterion by which their true value must be judged.

(8) The strategic problem of nuclear deterrence has a number of important consequences from the geographical point of view; to appreciate the significance of the resulting strategic interdependence factors which they produce, some knowledge of their evolution is necessary.

In the first phase nuclear deterrence depended upon aircraft with a limited radius of action; the deterrence system was therefore based upon a ring of peripheral air bases (sketch No. 1). From this sprang the air bases policy of the 1950's; it was a considerable factor in bringing the Americans and the Arab States closer together.

In the second phase, Soviet IRBMs appeared; the radius of action of these missiles was limited but they led, first to the down-grading

1. Peripheral air bases

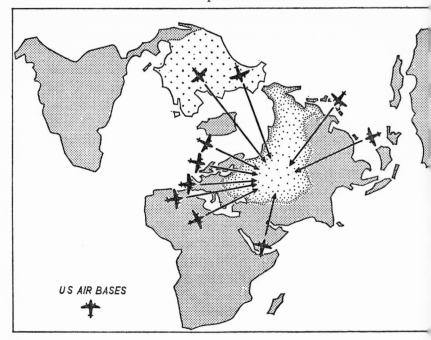

US AIR BASES

2. IRBM and air bases

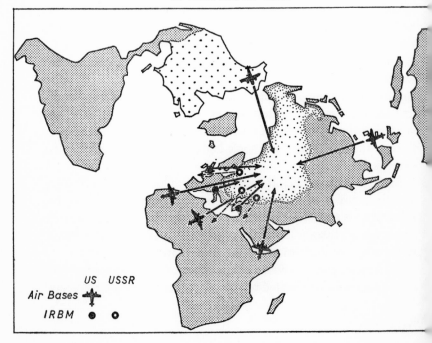

Air Bases

US   USSR

IRBM

of a certain number of the air bases as being too vulnerable and secondly to the setting up in Europe of a special theatre to meet the requirement for deployment of American IRBMs (sketch No. 2). It was at this period that missiles were installed in Great Britain, Italy and Turkey.

In the third phase, long-range missiles (ICBM) were developed; this focused attention once more on the direct mutual threat between the US and the USSR over the North Pole. The deployment of IRBM in Europe became a luxury of secondary importance (sketch No. 3). The deployment of IRBM in Cuba, on the other hand, was highly embarrassing to the United States and she went to great lengths to remove this threat.

In the fourth phase (the present) the development of missile carrying submarines has produced a new form of encirclement; but this time the encirclement is mutual and takes place on the high seas (sketch No. 4). From the geographical point of view, therefore, attention is now focused upon submarine bases (Great Britain, Spain, Cuba).

Each phase therefore was initiated by some highly important evolution producing a change in the relative strategic importance of the different areas. Similar changes have taken place in the field of advanced air warning and signal systems for transmission of alert messages. Technical considerations of this nature must be taken into account in any appreciation of the importance to either side of the various territories included in the Alliance and of their interdependence in the nuclear field.

CONCLUSION

The catchwords of direct deterrence strategy – and they are to a large extent contradictory – are therefore: increasingly complete but very localized and possibly precarious stability; complete identification of all powers with the nuclear deterrence system, which in the West must remain primarily American, but increased freedom of action thanks to this stability.

This being the environment, nations are in fact more free to act than they think but they face the risk that more serious conventional

3. IRBM and ICBM

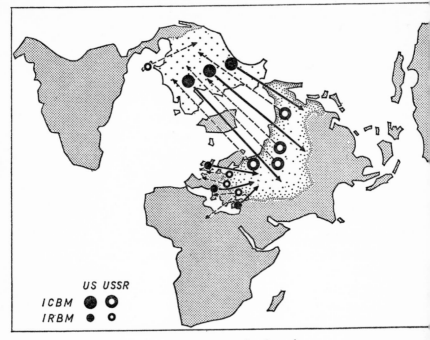

US USSR
ICBM ● ○
IRBM ● ○

4. IRBM, ICBM and submarines

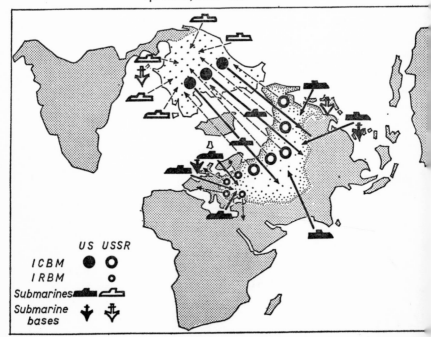

US USSR
ICBM ● ○
IRBM ● ○
Submarines
Submarine bases

conflicts may occur between non-nuclear powers in general or between nuclear powers in areas not covered by the nuclear freeze;
this freedom of action must therefore only be exercised with great
caution or the powers will find that they are sawing off the limb on
which they are sitting.

CONSEQUENCES OF DETERRENCE IN THE INDIRECT STRATEGY FIELD

We have seen that the particular characteristic of modern strategy
is that it prevents direct confrontation between the major military
powers and so opens up considerable freedom of action for the other
powers. *Our age is one of freedom of action in indirect strategy;*[1] this
means that we have freedom to encourage and exploit the natural
trend of the forces of change at work in the world. It is therefore
important to know what these natural trends are.

The natural trends

For too long now the world situation has been considered from the
standpoint of the great bipolar confrontation between the United
States and the USSR. This picture is an over-simplification and a
distortion of the truth; in fact the truth is far more complex. The
hallmark of the present day situation is that several major factors
are at work simultaneously.

1   *The fall of Europe* following two great wars; this has led first to
the collapse of the European world empire and secondly to a
vacuum in Central Europe, which the USSR has filled. The fall of
Europe therefore gives rise to two problems, the decolonization of
vast areas and Europe's own forcible division as a result of war; the
wound thus inflicted is barely healed and, together with the subjugation of the satellites, means that the germ of serious future
disease is still there. The Central European drama is typified by
Germany, herself divided.

Western Europe, nevertheless, has recovered both politically and
economically. From a military point of view, however, she is still
weak compared to her powerful neighbour, the USSR.

[1] And of paralysis of direct strategy particularly in the case of the nuclear powers.

K   145

2   *The elevation of the United States and the USSR* to the status of super-powers. The opposition between them has led them to take reciprocal precautionary measures in Europe and Asia. But the logic of the nuclear problem has forced them into a highly stable state of equilibrium militarily; this has now led them to establish between themselves a special relationship of a new type.

3   *The awakening of the 'Tiers Monde'*, springing from its contacts with European civilization. This was made possible by the collapse of Europe; it was accelerated by the political bidding match between the Americans and Russians and by the reciprocal neutralization produced by the nuclear equilibrium; it has been embittered by the old constraints of the colonial era.

The '*Tiers Monde*' leans both towards Europeanization and reversion to its ancient traditions; in its Europeanization it is undecided whether to adopt the Western or the Soviet pattern.

Some potential future giants are emerging from the '*Tiers Monde*', though still as yet more or less in their infancy: China, India, the Arab World. But the most general prospect is that of chaos, opening up considerable possibilities for indirect strategy action.

4   *The development of economic systems capable of producing goods in abundance* through the potentialities of modern technology.

This development has made possible the prosperity of America, the power of the Soviet Union and the rapid recovery of Europe; it stands out in sharp contrast to the conditions characteristic of the '*Tiers Monde*'; there technicians, capital and resources in general are in short supply, while the rapid expansion of population resulting from the miracle of modern medicine produces well-nigh insoluble problems. The gap between the two worlds is dangerous and growing.

To adapt itself to this new situation, the '*Tiers Monde*' may adopt either the liberal, the authoritarian or the Marxist technique, the latter revised in greater or lesser degree by the Chinese.

5   *The development of the Marxist ideology;* this has become a materialist interpretation and a secular version of Christian ideals; it has led to a messianic faith in historical evolution based on complete overthrow of certain long-established values, such as private

5. Geographical zones

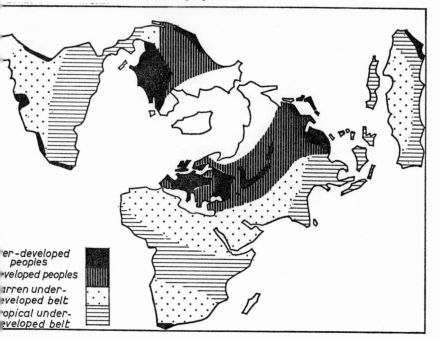

er-developed
  peoples
veloped peoples
arren under-
eveloped belt
ropical under-
eveloped belt

property, the profit motive, etc. This ideology, founded on nationalism and the proclaimed efficiency of Soviet or Chinese techniques, is tending to become the creed of the proletarian peoples.

6 *The appearance of the nuclear weapon* and more generally the invasion of the military technique by the achievements of science; this has led to the availability of means of destruction out of all proportion to the political aims of warfare. The results are a new equilibrium, still not complete, together with certain specific problems of considerable importance.

7 *The shrinkage of the world* as a result of modern techniques which have reduced distances and made rapid communication possible. The result is an almost complete *interdependence* between all peoples in the psychological and economic spheres as in the political and military.

8 *The geographical differences* dividing the world into four great zones (sketch No. 5):

147

Around the North Pole and halfway between it and the Equator, a temperate zone inhabited in general by the white race and by an almost continuous belt of peoples, highly developed or over-developed economically and united rather than divided by the Atlantic Ocean.

To the south of this zone, a more or less barren belt, often over-populated and under-developed, the Islamic area of Africa and the Middle East.

Further south again a tropical belt inhabited mostly by under-developed peoples of the black or yellow races and confined between the widely separated culs-de-sac of South America, Africa and Australia.

In Eastern Asia, China is a world of her own, straddling all three zones and contriving—with difficulty—to provide a living for one quarter of the human race.

Basic prospects

It is the combination of all these factors which determines the characteristics of the present day world and opens up a vista of the fundamentals of the future.

1   The economically developed zone is divided within itself by the great schism in Western civilization typified by the opposing ideologies which initially competed for Europe and are now competing for the '*Tiers Monde*'. These two opposing groups are engaged on a technological race which is a drain on their economies but a spur to rapid progress; through it they have achieved a military equilibrium, at the moment stable, which safeguards the *status quo* in Europe but is without effect upon the situation of the '*Tiers Monde*'.

As a result of this stability, the division of Europe and of Germany on the line agreed at Yalta has become dangerously congealed. An equitable settlement of the problems of Central Europe constitutes both the main danger and the primary cause of East-West tension.

There are three main ways in which this situation may develop.

It is not outside the bounds of possibility that the social and economic evolution of the West and the USSR may tend to reduce the differences which have sprung from the complete incompatibility of the two systems. Though starting from opposite extremes, socialist influences in the West, bourgeois influences in the USSR, may combine to produce not too dissimilar systems. The basic divergence of opinion on the matter of religion would remain but Providence will perhaps provide some solution to that. Pursuing this optimistic idea, the tension created by the Stalinist invasion of Central Europe and aggravated by the nuclear threat might then be resolved by an armistice halting the arms race and leading to an equitable revision of the state of affairs in Central Europe. European civilization with all its lights and shades would then be back on that road to unity from which it has strayed ever since 1914.

Alternatively, the subjugation of Central Europe, if maintained for too long, together with the liberal fever sweeping through Russia, may give rise to serious unrest in East Germany and the satellites; this would inevitably produce tensions highly dangerous for the peace of the world. Something like this is the most likely cause of open conflict. Such conflict need not necessarily be nuclear (it would probably not be) but it might have incalculable consequences.

Finally chance or the folly of man may bring a new Stalin to power in the USSR—or a new Hitler in Germany. In this event opposition between East and West would harden and its manifestations would be of the most violent nature, including the conquest of the '*Tiers Monde*', particularly Central and South America, with Cuba once more used as an offensive base. Although the intention might be to restrict action to indirect strategy methods, there would then be a direct threat to the under-belly of the United States, softened by racial tensions; because of the emotional reactions to which this would lead, it would be extremely dangerous. Pursuing this pessimistic line of thought, a major world conflict, probably nuclear, would be possible. It would bring about the final ruin of European civilization.

Of these three possibilities, the most desirable is clearly the first. It is to be feared, however, that it is unlikely to come about in its entirety, particularly as regards a *détente* in Central Europe, and that there will be many ups and downs, unless the threat of a re-emergent China acts as a spur.

2 The '*Tiers Monde*' of the barren and tropical zones, deprived of European guidance and in the throes of a population explosion, is wrestling with a host of difficult problems: how to create modern States without an adequate upper class: how to provide subsistence for a rapidly growing population without capital. Culturally, it is a frightening cauldron, splitting and coalescing at the whim of circumstances in the hope of reaching a European level of prosperity in the end.

Should this hope prove an illusion, all the ingredients are there for a new and gigantic *Völkerwanderung* perhaps towards the turn of the century, threatening the developed areas of Europe and America. If, on the other hand, the uncommitted world tries to raise itself out of its age-long misery, it will give birth to new powers, both economic and military, and they, with the brutality of newly emerged peoples, will strive to lay hands on the riches of the temperate zone. In either case, therefore, towards the turn of the century, the economically highly developed areas of the world must be prepared for a severe struggle in defence of their existence and their freedoms.

It would be a tragedy if, at that time, this threatened world were still divided against itself. In all probability it would go under.

3 Earlier than this, however, *Communist China* will present a special problem, because with her natural resources, the qualities of her people, and the size of her population, she should be able to make more rapid progress – a later edition, in fact, of that made by the USSR.

If in, say, fifteen years, the USSR and a powerful rehabilitated China were to be found side by side in the same Communist camp, this would be a danger of the first order for the West. The West would then no longer be able to stem the tide by concentric action in Asia, the Pacific, or even in the Middle East and Africa. The '*Tiers Monde*', including South America, economically still to a large extent in the colonial era, would be lost. Fortunately a number of factors tend to drive the two great Marxist neighbours into opposition; these factors are geo-political, ideological (China, an age-old non-Christian Empire, is more likely than Russia to develop an ant-like civilization) and even racial.

The pressure of China, already foreseen by the USSR, is a long-term danger to the West, but in the short term it is the only possible counterweight holding out any hope of peaceful settlement of the Central European problems now dividing the West and the USSR.

For both these reasons we should make every effort to avoid throwing China into the arms of the USSR and we should draw what advantage we can from the opposition between them.

4 *Europe.* Though still convalescent and divided, Europe since the loss of her Colonial Empire forms a compact densely populated entity; with her diversity and dynamism she is the repository and ever fertile crucible of ancient western civilization. The tempest of the Second World War in large measure removed the mainsprings of those aggressive tendencies which sprang from the old nationalist particularism. Mass production techniques (the new god of the doctrine of material wellbeing), a certain tendency to ape America, and nostalgia for the world-power status, which the present day nations of Europe no longer possess, have given rise to the hope of a united Europe able to play a role analogous to that of the United States, the USSR, and in the future China.

This vision would perhaps have been easier to achieve fifteen years ago amid the ruins of war; today, when the nation states have been re-formed into powerful entities, it comes up against the obstacle of their divergent interests. If it comes to pass at all, it can do so only through a system preserving, possibly for a long time to come, the present national entities; their history is too rich and their civilization too distinctive for them to sink their identities in a single unifying mould. Europe may perhaps achieve her initial unity on the Swiss model, but not on that of Germany or Italy. Insofar as technical activities are concerned however – and that includes the organization of her defence, in particular the vital end-of-the-century problem – there would be many advantages in a progressive co-ordination followed by integration, so that Europe might form an entity commensurate with the present scale of world affairs.

But the unification of Europe faces four great problems.

The first, with us now, is that of the powers to be grouped together to form the core of the future structure. In 1946, following

Churchill's line of thought, United Europe could have been born by drawing tighter the bonds between France and Great Britain. Many affinities, many similarities and many memories shared were there to justify the concept. But apart from the basic isolationism stemming from the British insular and imperial traditions, the great difference of outlook lay in the fact that Great Britain has never known foreign occupation of her territory, and so has never had to wrestle with the profound upheavals which go therewith. So it would seem, that in spite of its age-long divergencies but because of recent experiences shared in common, it is from the Continent of Europe that united Europe must emerge; it must be done by drawing tighter the bonds between France, Germany and Italy, and, if possible, the Benelux countries. But very soon, as soon as 'fermentation' starts, to this core of Europe must be added the contributions of the British, Scandinavian, Spanish, Greek and even Turkish branches of the European family.

At the latest when this happens, we shall be faced with the second problem (already referred to above), that of Central Europe; there can be no United Europe without Austria, Poland, Roumania, Czechoslovakia, Hungary, Yugoslavia and Bulgaria. 'Reconquest' is unthinkable, and a process of prising them loose from the Soviet grip is conceivable only in an atmosphere of *détente* such that no suspicion of a Russian defeat would be implied.

This thought is at the root of the hopes some Europeans on both sides of the Iron Curtain place in a neutralist policy. Though it has many attractions, a homeopathic policy of this nature would seem to present more disadvantages than advantages, the most serious problem being the fact that German unity would be achieved under the aegis of the USSR; in that event we should be giving to the United States exactly that feeling of defeat which we might congratulate ourselves on having avoided in the case of the Soviet Union. Europe would in effect have opted out of the Western camp and this could not but push the United States back into isolationism, leaving Europe alone to face the might of the Soviet Union. If, on the other hand, neutralization of Europe took place under the joint patronage of the United States and the USSR, this would inevitably bring the Americans and Russians closer together. In this case a 'neutral' Europe would in effect risk being governed by a Russo-American 'condominium'. The independence policy recently inaugurated by France may in fact be very different from what we think, if it serves to emphasize the European nature of European initiatives and differentiates them from those of the United States; this is, of course, subject to the proviso that it does not break up the military alliance which remains essential to deterrence and politically is required to hold and reassure Western Germany. The path is narrow and difficult, for it involves numerous contradictions, and we must neither bewilder nor discourage the United States. Nevertheless the French initiative may point the way to a solution from which will emerge that delicate but essential evolution towards a Europe stretching 'from the Atlantic to the Vistula', closely linked defensively to the United States but with no further claims against the USSR. We must act quickly, for the moment of decision in Central Europe may come soon.

The third problem, allied to the first two, is the provision for Europe of some status in its own right as a strategic entity, in other words promoting it to the rank of a nuclear power. A great deal has been written on this subject. There is no need here to go into all its ramifications but it is legitimate to wonder how 'independent' a Europe would be if its security depended entirely upon agreement between the United States and the USSR. This would, in fact, be an unavowed 'condominium' situation. Conversely the idea of an independent but non-nuclear Europe only makes sense if one accepts the American theory that any not strictly bipolar nuclear system is too dangerous. I hope that I have demonstrated the fallacy of this theory in Part One of this book. Arrangements such as the Multilateral Force, the object of which is to maintain the bipolar system, while giving Europe an illusion that she is participating, do not of course stand up to examination. Sooner or later, therefore, Europe must become nuclear or renounce its freedom. But she cannot become a nuclear power until she exists as a political entity, and that may take so long that we on this side of the Atlantic may have fallen irretrievably behind in the race. For this reason the efforts made by Great Britain and France to develop an embryo nuclear capability may prove of value, even though neither can hope to reach the level of the super-powers; these forces may be the essential forerunners of a future European force.

The fourth problem is that facing Europe now that she controls only the northern shore of the Mediterranean. Should Northern Africa unite and become in any degree hostile, Europe would see the resurgence of a danger which has appeared throughout history under the various guises of Carthage, the Moorish Empire, and the Ottoman Empire. Europe, now looking eastwards, would then have to turn south. Decolonization notwithstanding, this possibility forces Europe to coordinate her action in this area, for it is of immediate and vital interest to her security.

5 A further possibility for unity has now appeared. Unity within the *Atlantic framework*. This implies that on either side of the Atlantic (the Mediterranean of our shrunken world) peoples born of the same civilization should form a community. This is a worthy object and is no doubt one of the most likely possibilities in the very long term.

The value of the proposal depends entirely upon its scope and the extent of unification envisaged. Had it been brought about some years ago and had it been limited to Europe (this was in fact impossible because of the colonial implications), it would have produced a swarm of satellite states bound to the United States and governed in fact from Washington. Kennedy put forward another better balanced solution, that of the 'twin pillars', 'equal partners' in the Alliance. This solution presupposes that a real and sufficiently reunified Europe exists, seemingly the minimum prerequisite for any system of Atlantic 'Union'. Nevertheless a scheme such as this, feasible only in the long term, seems at this stage to be somewhat narrow and bearing too clear an imprint of present-day difficulties. When only two parties are involved, a balanced 'union' is difficult. Taking the most optimistic view, is it not legitimate to hope that this Atlantic 'Union' might include South America (if it was not too late) and even in the extreme case, and provided the necessary conditions could be fulfilled, the USSR? In that event it would really be a community based on European civilization, reuniting to Europe its Western and Eastern off-shoots. Such an idea, put forward today, may surprise and even shock some people, but let it not be forgotten that we were allied to the Russians only twenty years ago when Stalin was in power and the ideological differences were even greater than they are today. Let us not also forget that nuclear strategy produces a powerful community of interest tending towards a sort of world condominium of the United States and the USSR. The only way of avoiding the disadvantages inherent in such a situation while at the same time profiting from the stability – and the economy – which a definite *détente* between East and West would produce, is ourselves to be a member of this concert of powers. Such a situation would inevitably take time to evolve, and it is not inconceivable that by that time the USSR, prosperous and under pressure from a China by then dangerous, would be ready to join the Western family without introducing too disturbing an element of disharmony.

The Atlantic community would then be ready to face the dangers of the year 2000.

CONCLUSION

The main possibilities would, therefore, appear to be the following:
1 *In the short term* a high degree of nuclear stability which will require considerable care and continuous effort to maintain; it should, however, make a nuclear catastrophe or major upheaval in Europe improbable. This will contrast with a high degree of instability in the '*Tiers Monde*' which is plagued by grievous growing pains and will be a source of reiterated conflict.

The situation will, therefore, be partly congealed and partly fluid; it will offer a high degree of freedom of action to indirect strategy, tempered, however, by the close nuclear, political and economic interdependence of the globe as a whole, now a single theatre of operations.

2 *In the medium term*, the emergence of China as an important international factor; possible results are:

Either that she will ally herself closely with the USSR; in that case the communist bloc will constitute a formidable force able to assert its predominance over the '*Tiers Monde*'; the great cleavage in European civilization will be perpetuated:

Or that she will stand in opposition to the USSR; in this case a certain degree of world equilibrium will be re-established. This will assist in reconstituting the unity of European civilization; it should be possible gradually to solve the problems of Central Europe.

3 *In the long term* formidable prospects for the highly developed world resulting from the probable evolution of the '*Tiers Monde*'.

In parallel with this it is conceivable that the great cleavage in European civilization will be healed by the formation of a widespread community of continents; Europe, the kernel of this system, will be formed into a coherent, though disparate, entity, almost certainly on the Swiss model, and including those peoples of the East to whom she is traditionally linked by history.

OUTLINE OF A WORLD STRATEGY

Although the foregoing analysis has been confined to problems of a strategic nature, it has necessarily been based to a considerable extent upon forecasts of a political nature. In working out a world strategy the political angle will be even more important, for strategy after all is nothing but the art of using force to contribute to the attainment of the ends fixed by policy. Where do we want to get? This opens up the whole problem of our long-term political objective.

The long-term political objective

Decision upon this objective is a problem of politics not strategy. It is not therefore within the scope of the present study. From a strategic point of view we need only note that it is a pity that such an objective has never been laid down by the West other than in vague and often contradictory terms. The reasons are known to us all: divergencies of view between the United States and the former colonial powers, propaganda arguments, the illusion that all problems, particularly those of the '*Tiers Monde*', could be solved simultaneously.

The civilization of the third millennium is now germinating in a shrunken and over-populated world, of which the hallmarks are productivity and technology. Clearly the great problem is to know what sort of civilization this will be, and in what measure our precious Greco-Latin and Christian traditions will be preserved and properly exploited.

From this point of view it would seem that the object of any top-level policy worthy of the name must be the harmonious development of our civilization (but what civilization? – this is the crucial problem with which I shall not deal here), while at the same time employing aid effectively to stave off the growing pauperization of the '*Tiers Monde*'.

Correspondingly it will be accepted that essentials are the cohesion and prosperity of Europe and the Atlantic World (but what do these words mean? – here is another vital political problem).

These are the sort of political options on which a long-term choice must be made; I have given them here merely as examples, but only in the light of the choice made can the strategy be laid down.

The strategic objectives

On the assumption that these ideas, which I have designedly kept in general terms, are accepted as a basis, we can now go on to pick out the main strategic objectives which would flow from this concept.

1   The first and unarguable strategic objective is to avoid the great nuclear conflict between the USSR and the United States. Although it has been shown that such a conflict is improbable at the moment, it remains possible under certain circumstances, against which we must be on our guard. One, and the most vital, would be Russo-Chinese collaboration, another the premature disintegration of the Atlantic Alliance, yet another some serious incident in Central Europe resulting from pressures being allowed to build up for too long. The *détente* is therefore to the good insofar as it does not carry with it the risk of one of the above developments. For instance too early a rapprochement between the United States and the USSR would involve danger of freezing the Yalta line and destroying the Atlantic Alliance. At the other end of the scale a bold policy of aid

to China may, from certain points of view, prove a stabilizing factor.

2 The second objective, allied to the first but of even wider consequence, is the search for a world system of maximum stability.

Laudable attempts have been made to produce it through juridical systems such as the League of Nations and UNO but they have not stood up to major storms. The reality of the inhibitions produced by a world opinion in favour of peace should not be underestimated, but it must be admitted that at the present stage UNO is not capable of dealing with anything other than minor crises. It is still no more than a contributory factor and its peace-keeping value is largely offset by the fact that it offers a sounding-board for the passions of the least educated peoples with consequent disturbing effects. For a long time to come force is bound to remain an essential element in stability. For this reason a policy of disarmament or even control of armaments may prove highly dangerous unless geared to the maintenance of deterrence.

Nuclear weapons, studied at length in this book, are the key to stability because of the mutual danger they produce. But as we have seen, for reasons still only partially understood, the influence of their power extends only over certain areas of the globe. Because of the instability still existing in other areas and because the various problems are interdependent, the risk remains that conflicts may arise and that they may spread. So, as we stand at present, nuclear weapons are only a partial, and therefore inadequate, answer.

The present day world has so far been based upon a bipolar equilibrium between the United States and the USSR. This is the *de facto* position resulting from the situation at the end of the war; in view of the dynamic of international affairs, it may be thought to be the least stable: here are two great powers surrounded by their groups of satellites; the smallest conflict involving two of their hangers-on would bring the two face to face. History shows that situations such as this, in which two great expanding powers are opposed, have never produced stable equilibrium. By a sort of fatal law of gravity, one of the two has always ended by destroying the other, unless their energies have been diverted and tempered by the influence of counterbalancing coalitions.

The fact is that unless there are specific favourable conditions, such as those analysed under the various levels of deterrence, the basis of international stability is the tendency automatically to support the weaker side, or even to take his place should he fall. This is what happened, for instance, in 1940 when the fall of Poland followed by that of France did not result in a German victory; the running was taken up first by Great Britain, then America and then the Soviet Union. The best guarantee of security is the prospect faced by an aggressor of seeing the number of his potential enemies increase the greater his success becomes; he must therefore have a number of partners, in other words the world must be truly multipolar. Only then will it be possible to make the regroupings of forces required to preserve the balance, if necessary take the edge off over-dangerous expansionism by minor conflict, and so avoid general war. This is the doctrine which has governed European policy for centuries; it would now be worth applying it at world level.

For this purpose it is clearly desirable that new powerful entities should be formed. NATO was the first of these counterbalancing coalitions; the reply to NATO was the Warsaw Pact and probably Bandoeng. But the purpose of these arrangements is a restricted one (defensive in the case of NATO and the Warsaw Pact); they are not, therefore, powers in the strict sense of the word. To reach balance through a multipolar world structure necessitates at the very least the constitution of Europe as a coherent and distinct entity, and the recovery of China. The formation of a United Europe of world-power status is therefore an imp´rtant factor in stability.

This raises the question whether a united Europe should be considered as one of the 'twin pillars' of an Atlantic system or as a possible third force between the United States and the USSR. The question has already been dealt with; there can be no flat answer to it; defensively Europe should be linked closely to the United States through the Atlantic Alliance, but the relationship must be tempered by a marked degree of political independence, and as Europe becomes more solidly constituted, it should evolve towards military autonomy.

3 But this concept of a more balanced and articulated world than the present makes it more necessary than ever to organize *a*

good system of coordination of the strategies of the West. This must undoubtedly be the third objective of any sound world strategy.

Up to now the Atlantic Alliance's direct strategy for the defence of Europe has been very closely controlled by the United States, whereas outside the NATO area indirect strategy has been conducted by each of the Allies entirely independently of each other and in a generally inconsistent manner. On the one side there has been over-centralization and on the other almost complete anarchy. In the light of the importance of indirect strategy and the change in the balance brought about by the political and economic recovery of Europe, some more equitable and more efficient system must be found.

This is what the French Government proposed as early as November 1958; no true answer has ever been given to its memorandum. The two points raised were control of world strategy and nuclear strategy. These two points are still crying out for solution.

(a) *In the direct strategy field*, the principle of collective control of strategy has been accepted in theory, but in fact has been completely by-passed as far as nuclear strategy is concerned; the latter has so far been considered by the Americans as a strictly national matter, whereas in fact it forms the foundation of the common strategy of NATO. NATO competence can no longer be restricted to the limited problems of the tactical defence of Europe within a strategic framework laid down outside the Alliance. On the nuclear level this problem is facing us now, owing to the appearance of the French independent nuclear force. But in fact, as knowledge of the strategic realities develops among the various nations of Europe, it will become a problem facing the Alliance as a whole.

Post-1960 evolution in American thinking in this field has tended to complicate the problem rather than resolve it. The Americans have laid emphasis upon two considerations which they consider basic: fear of nuclear proliferation, and the necessity for completely centralized nuclear control. But these two points are only partially valid and there are other at least equally important considerations.

The basic error was the belief that politically it would be

possible to maintain indefinitely the complete hegemony exercised by the United States in nuclear matters, and that from the material point of view it would be possible to prevent France completing her nuclear programme.

This error has blinded people to the alternative solutions which sooner or later will become essential.

Moreover, as we have already seen,[1] the fact that the allies of the United States (except perhaps Great Britain) have not been able to follow in detail the evolution of American ideas on the nuclear weapon has produced a dangerous intellectual gap; this shows itself in differences of appreciation, which would in many cases have been avoided had the problems been studied in concert in years past.

The construction of an allied nuclear strategy raises two problems; the first is theoretical, that of the role of allied and independent nuclear forces; the second is practical, that of the possibility of coordination of allied nuclear strategies.

The role of an allied and independent nuclear force has been fairly exhaustively studied in Part One.[2] I hope that I have proved sufficiently convincingly that the existence of such a force may give more flexibility and more effect to allied deterrent action, while at the same time increasing solidarity.

I also indicated how the mutual education of the partners in the Alliance might be achieved in order to ensure satisfactory co-ordination of their deterrent strategies.

Naturally, the necessary organizations will have to be set up. Some for the *study and preparation phase* (of the type no doubt of the Berlin Quadripartite Group), others for the *coordination of the deterrent manœuvre* (what the Americans term 'crisis management'); the latter will require signal systems enabling heads of government and their military headquarters to be in constant and instantaneous communication with each other. There would be no question of restricting the freedom of the various participants, still less of giving anyone the right of veto; the object would be to produce concerted and well prepared decisions.

---

[1] See Chapter Three, 'Multilateral Deterrence'.
[2] Ibid.

Naturally also preparation would be made for the coordinated *use* of force to meet the highly improbable case when deterrence had failed; but as has been emphasized above, action must be considered from the angle of deterrence, not from that of the use of force.

The problem in fact, therefore, is to find some method of producing a truly collective system of direction instead of restricting allied action to the operational problems of local defence in the European theatre. The fact that nuclear strategy has evolved from one of defence to one of deterrence, makes this change absolutely essential, while the formation of independent nuclear forces compels us to organize their coordination.

Present day prejudices notwithstanding, it does seem that a multipolar nuclear system based upon a common concept and so bringing the various allied initiatives into harmony, might produce a more complete and more stable deterrent effect than a strictly bipolar system. The necessary organization can perfectly well be designed. Moreover, more detailed analysis would show that the difference between the coordination found necessary on the conventional level (for Berlin for instance) and that which must now be achieved at the nuclear level, is a difference of degree and not of kind.

Finally, as we have already seen, if these necessities were recognized together with the very real advantages they might produce, the present obstacles to technical osmosis between the allies would be removed, and the Alliance as a whole would get a very much greater dividend from the considerable expenditure it devotes to armaments.

(b) *In the indirect strategy field*, where the contest is on a world scale and conducted by cold war or semi-hot war methods, it is essential to re-establish a minimum of cohesion if the West is to regain the initiative, for in indirect strategy the initiative is the prime factor.

There being no question of diluting national sovereignty, there were three possible solutions:

Anarchy, resulting in uncoordinated action.

Consultation within NATO.

Formulation of a common strategy, if possible.

This last was the solution proposed by the French Government. It was not adopted, and so a system of consultation within NATO was tried; this never really functioned, and could in any case hardly produce practical results seeing that within NATO interest in extra-European questions differs considerably and is frequently divergent. We therefore reverted to uncoordinated action, the disadvantages of which are obvious.

The only logical solution, difficult to achieve though it may be, is to revert to discussion of a common strategy between those nations having world-wide interests and then to proceed to apply this strategy regionally, in discussion with those allied nations concerned. This presupposes that a suitable organization exists.[1]

Some people may say that France's recent behaviour is proof that the freedom of action resulting from the present anarchy allows people to exploit their opportunities in a manner which would hardly be permissible in a collective system of any sort. The fact that on occasions one must take the initiative to get things out of a rut is no argument against a system of coordination; on the contrary, under such a system these initiatives should be the result of discriminating and concerted team work.

Probably we have a long way to go in this matter, for minds are still not adjusted to solutions of this type. It must be realized, however, that the adjustments the West must make to ensure better cohesion can only be in this direction. If this is not done, Western global initiatives run the risk of becoming less and less coordinated, and therefore dangerously divergent.

CONCLUSIONS

This analysis based on the three great fundamental strategic objectives, brings out a number of practical medium-term and short-term consequences; they confirm and put in order the majority of

---

[1] The remarkable work done on Berlin is an interesting precedent, and shows the lines on which a practical solution might be found.

the conclusions drawn from our study of factors governing direct deterrent strategy and indirect strategy.

The picture which emerges is inevitably highly complex, but certain essential features stand out clearly:

The major long-term danger which may come from the '*Tiers Monde*' and the consequent necessity to move towards as large as possible a community of peoples whose roots lie in European civilization, now in process of rejuvenation.

The major medium-term importance of giving the world a more stable structure based upon a multipolar system; correspondingly, the necessity for formation of a United Europe and the basic advantages of an emergent China, provided she is not tied to the USSR; the necessity for a timely and equitable solution of the problems of Central Europe.

In the short term, the need for the stability given us by the Atlantic Alliance, the organization and internal balance of which must be improved; at the same time, the requirement for closer Western cohesion in the field of indirect strategy in order to avoid the more dangerous of the errors already visible – in particular those of forcing China into close alliance with the USSR, missing the opportunity for effective aid to the uncommitted world and so allowing a dangerous discontent to fester, bringing about a premature rapprochement between the United States and the USSR to the detriment of Western cohesion and of any improvement in the situation in Central Europe.

All that I have said above deals only with the strategic aspect of the consequences of deterrence. Let me emphasize once more that this aspect alone is not enough to justify this or that conclusion: a policy giving first priority to the integration of Europe into the United States would lead to very different consequences from one giving priority to the formation of United Europe. Still other consequences would emerge if the object was a Europe devoted to the Atlantic ideal or designed to play the role of a third force. Depending upon the object in view, the existence of an independent nuclear force, however useful it may be strategically, may be impossible or harmful or indispensable politically.

The table opposite shows in summary form and as an example

STRATEGIC CONSEQUENCES

CONDITIONS

Rapprochement USSR–US	Rapprochement USSR–China	United Europe	Central Europe Liberation	Central Europe Status quo	Central Europe Coordinated Strategy	Atlantic Alliance	Political Decision	Nuclear Force Independent	Nuclear Force European	Nuclear Force Atlantic	Atlantic Alliance	Coordinated Strategy	Aid to China	Aid to 'Tiers Monde'	Disarmament
—	+	—	—	+	—	+	Atlantic Union +satellites.	—	—	+	+	—	—	+	—
?	—	+	—	+	+	+	Atlantic Union twin pillars.	+	+	—	+	+	+	+	—
?	—	+	+	—	+	+	Atlantic Community 3–4 pillars.	+	+	—	+	+	+	+	?
+	—	?	?	?	—	+	US–USSR Condominium.	—	—	+	—	—	—	+	+
—	+	—	—	+	—	+	Bipolar world.	—	—	+	+	—	—	+	—
?	—	+	+	—	+	+	Multipolar world.	+	+	—	+	+	+	+	?
⧺	—	+	+	—	+	+	No nuclear war.	+	+	—	+	+	+	+	—
⧺	—	+	+	—	+	+	More stable world.	+	+	—	+	+	+	+	—
—	—	+	?	?	+	+	Coordinated strategies.	+	+	—	+	+	+	+	?
?	—	+	+	—	+	—	Europe as third force.	+	+	—	—	+	+	+	—

165

only, the conditions justifying various political decisions and the possible effects these decisions will have upon the main factors in strategy.

A similar table could be made for the various political decisions concerning (e.g.) Europe or Africa.

It will be seen that these various political decisions stem from very differing conditions and produce very differing strategic consequences. Nevertheless one or two constants stand out: the Atlantic Alliance is indispensable except in the case of a US–USSR condominium or Europe as a third force; aid to the uncommitted world is necessary under all circumstances. There are two broadly similar families of solutions: a family of policies envisaging, with various shades of emphasis, a bipolar world, and a family of policies envisaging a multipolar world; the results of the latter are similar to those of policies aiming at peace and stability. But it will be noted, for instance, that any permanent rapprochement between China and the USSR entails the maintenance of a bipolar world. Finally, large-scale disarmament hardly appears possible except in the condominium case.

This is doubtless all too systematized, but it does give some idea of the close relationship existing between political decisions and strategic desiderata.

2 OVERALL CONCLUSIONS ON WORLD STRATEGY

The body of considerations and deductions in this chapter is an attempt to bring together into a single process of reasoning the main strategic problems of our era; it also aims to show what sort of mechanism is required to discover the various solutions required and to ensure that they have some rational foundation and are based upon strategic factors. I am under no illusions as to the difficulties and indeed the audacity of this undertaking; for the sake of brevity I have plunged in with both feet and disregarded many of the nuances. Moreover, I repeat yet again that I have had to avoid becoming involved in strictly political arguments, although I have not been able to help trespassing considerably into this field. Such as it is, and in spite of the reservations I have made here, my analysis will undoubtedly give rise to numerous objections.

I have decided nevertheless to put forward this analysis *as an illustration only*, for I believe that this type of intellectual exercise, imperfect though it may be and even though it includes errors as this one probably does, is an indispensable basis for any decision, and so for each of the strategic decisions which have to be taken daily as circumstances demand. As I said in my *Introduction to Strategy*: 'Our age is too difficult and man has attained too great a mastery over nature for us to go on working by the light of nature as we have already done for too long . . . Our civilization requires a science of taking action . . . a "praxeology".' In such a science strategy could and should play a key role; it should be strategy which ensures that decisions taken to further a certain policy are conscious fully thought-out decisions. That is the object which any examination of strategy should seek to attain. This is what I have tried to explain in this chapter by showing how the various factors act and what is the principal inter-relationship in logic between the various developments.

Strategy will then be seen to be a *prospectus for action*, continuous action at the present time taken within the framework of a forecast concept of overall future evolution; its object is to contribute to certain possible situations rather than others, the choice being a political one. I would even go so far as to say that according to this concept strategy is the only practicable 'prospectus' for it seeks not to *guess* what the future will be but to *build* the future methodically taking as its starting point that which one wishes to achieve and that which appears to be feasible.

The future cannot be discerned because it is contingent upon so many factors, but it does to a certain extent depend upon the intelligence and the will of man. So far, man's intelligence and man's will have manifested themselves primarily by action on a level which is no more than microcosmic when considered in relation to mankind as a whole. Scientific discoveries, intellectual and technical advances have destroyed the equilibrium automatically established during the slow evolution of previous eras. The sum total of action at the microcosmic level has produced formidable phenomena at the macrocosmic level – at global level in other words; they have been neither foreseen nor directed. Man's intelligence and man's will must therefore now be applied at the macrocosmic level if he is to regain a degree of control over his destiny.

I once heard an intellectual (he was British) say that no political decision had ever been taken other than under the immediate pressure of events and that the philosophers were the only people who thought of the future. This sally was no doubt exaggerated, but unfortunately it contains a considerable element of truth. Our traditional methods of reaching decisions have quite clearly become impracticable today. We cannot go on groping our way forward as we did in a stable world (though that world, be it noted, was periodically the scene of major catastrophes). The basic point is that any future catastrophe will now be of our own making, and that we undoubtedly have the power to avoid it. Humanity has emerged from its long childhood and is now adult, in other words it is now fully responsible for its own destiny. In Marx's view this destiny was to be moulded by technology and economics That is only part of the problem. At the macrocosmic level other formidable factors come into play and they are factors upon which strategy can exert a rational influence. This is what I have been trying to show; I have not been advocating this or that solution. Thanks to strategy we should now be able, as day-to-day events in all their diversity crowd in upon us, to work out the short-term decision best calculated to achieve the long-term object we shall have set ourselves as the result of careful study of all the various prospects. The quicker you go, the further ahead you must look.

But all – or nearly all – of what I have set out in this chapter constitutes only the strategic part of the problem. It is only one side of the dialogue between the strategist and the politician. This dialogue is necessary, but it would be very serious if it led strategy to dominate policy (as sometimes seems to happen in the United States). Strategic arguments, however important they may be today, are no more than one of the factors in a political decision, a factor which answers the question 'how' and which may therefore, to a certain extent, influence the answer to the question 'what', by ensuring that it remains within the realm of possibility.

The answer to the vital question 'what' must emerge from quite another field of thought, basically of a philosophical nature. So long as man refuses to make an adequate effort in this field, to make up his mind where he really wishes to go, he will continue to be the plaything of those colossal forces which he has unwittingly released in his blind search for immediate material advantage.

Conclusions

So here we are at the end of this study of the nature and consequences of deterrence. Any reader who has had the patience to go
through it all cannot fail to recognize the diversity of the vistas
it opens up or the importance of the conclusions to which it
leads.

I propose to set out here only those conclusions I consider basic.
Although they may appear trite or bordering on the self-evident, I
have a feeling that all too often they do not figure adequately in our
concepts on strategy and international relations.

(1) The disproportionate dangers produced by nuclear weapons
have now become such that it is very difficult to conceive of open
war in the areas where a minimum of credibility still attaches to the
use of nuclear weapons.

As a result, in these areas the role of armed forces, and in particular nuclear forces, must not be considered from the point of view
of their possible employment in war, as has been our habit, but
from that of the prevention of war, in other words of *deterrence*.

(2) This fundamental transformation in the character and influence
of armaments entails an almost complete *reversal* of our concepts:
the danger of destruction creates stability, too great stability re-
creates the danger (of war). So the subtle rules of a new game of
international relationships begin to emerge with increasing clarity:
the object of the game is to maintain deterrent effect by a judicious
admixture of danger and stability. It is a form of strategy, the
strategy of deterrence.

(3) The essential feature of the strategy of deterrence, dissected at length in this book, lies in the non-employment of nuclear weapons through judicious exploitation of the fact that they exist. Although deterrence cannot be classed as an operation of war, it is – contrary to some beliefs – neither policy nor diplomacy. It is a powerful instrument, *at the disposal of policy*: it is a strategy.

(4) Since, like any other strategy, it must be subordinate to policy, the strategy of deterrence can only produce meaningful solutions in the light of the political aim being pursued. As in any argument between the strategist and the politician, the strategist can do no more than emphasize the limits of his capabilities and recommend the solutions which appear to him the most favourable; it is for the politician to decide in the light of his wider spectrum of considerations.

(5) Since the strategy of deterrence does not make actual use of its weapons, technical developments play a less decisive role than in a war strategy. The technical qualities of weapons are of course important, but their psychological and political impact is so overriding that it largely outweighs the technical aspect; thus the French strategic force exerted an influence well before it was actually in existence. The strategy of deterrence is therefore far more abstract and ambiguous than the strategy of war.

These conclusions show up some of the main characteristics of our era; they deserve to be recognized and distinguished from the political element, which forms one of their ingredients.

On the other hand, political factors as such being excluded from this study, though it has been possible to tackle the majority of the great strategic problems of the day, it has not been possible to reach definite or complete conclusions upon them: the objective has been lacking. Everything in fact depends upon the political aim being pursued. If the British, for instance, regarded their nuclear force merely as an instrument to guarantee them a certain international standing and to maintain their 'special relationship' with the United States, there would be nothing to prevent them placing their national force under NATO orders and accepting the 'sub-strategic' task of interdiction in defence of the European theatre. If the object of neutral Sweden was simply to reinforce her defences and threaten a potential invader with nuclear escalation, tactical nuclear weapons would be by far her best solution; they would be easier and less expensive to produce and militarily more effective than a purely conventional defence. If, on the other hand, France's purpose was not only to underline her independence in order to obtain a better balance in the control of NATO, but to establish her case for a 'special relationship' with the United States and pave the way for an embryo European nuclear force, she had to have as modern as possible a strategic force component. The political objective is decisive.

The 'great debate' on these problems should therefore in the first instance be a debate on the political objective. Only in the light of this objective and by comparing the anticipated advantages with their cost and their risks, can one hope to reach a conclusion. On the strategical plane alone, and still more on the technical plane, we cannot be in possession of all the decisive factors affecting these problems.

Though this study has designedly been restricted to the strategic aspect, I have tried to make a careful analysis of the strictly military consequences of the deterrent phase through which we are now passing. The problem has been to look for, and bring out into the open, some logical basis for the role to be allotted today to military forces, now that their use would appear to be generally restricted to the minor forms of warfare.

The logical basis would appear to a great extent to emerge from the essential distinction we have drawn between the forms of warfare for which preparations are made in order that they may be used, and those for which preparations are made in order to prevent them being used. The resulting train of thought should lead to the establishment of the principles governing a nuclear age defence doctrine; but with this goes the necessity to be prepared at any time to adapt oneself to very different types of action by preparing simultaneously for two types of war at opposite ends of the scale – limited conventional war and 'spasm' nuclear war.

These principles should help to give us back our confidence, all too often lacking in this field owing to the accumulation of contra-dictions and over-simplifications. The nuclear weapon has brought profound changes to the methods employed in the defence function but the function as such still has all its old importance. In fact, since the total strategy of deterrence is constantly in action, the defence function has also become a continuous operation instead of being restricted as in the old days to periods of serious crisis.

Let us hope that our military professionals will grasp this new truth and so come to realize that their day-to-day efforts have some meaning and value.

Looking further ahead than our present day problems, considera-tion of deterrence brings out certain major conclusions opening up a vista of new developments.

(1) An extraordinary transformation has taken place in the modern world; the cauldron is seething as a result of the impact of techno-logy, the new White Man's magic, and of the collapse of the European World Empire; the '*Tiers Monde*' is frantically European-izing itself and over everything tower the American and Russian giants. It is all in a state of flux.

Nevertheless at the same time the nuclear weapon introduces a completely new factor of stability. Wherever its influence extends the situation congeals, whereas outside its influence the pace of upheaval increases (Asia and Africa are on the move, but Berlin and Formosa are stagnant). One of the most important questions facing us is to find out whether in fact it is possible to extend nuclear stability to other zones and so put a brake on the more dangerous developments. It seems possible that such a prospect may open up through the machinery of multilateral deterrence, so far regarded from too narrow a point of view, that of fear and the interests of the two great nuclear powers.

(2) Another major conclusion is inescapable. We are in the midst of events, the evolution of which we have not so far been able to foresee, and in which all forecasts prove precarious. It is vital that we should know how we intend to bring some conscious influence to bear on the future. Irrespective of the philosophical or political line we choose to follow, we are therefore faced with the problem of

the *manœuvre in time*. This would seem to be the essential role of modern strategy, just as the manœuvre in space was that of traditional strategy.

Some of the points raised in our study of the strategic consequences of deterrence and the necessity for an adaptable military system give an indication of what a rational solution might be: we must set out the whole gamut of possible long-term hypotheses in order to be ready to intervene in the short term, so as to ensure that of all the hypotheses proved valid, the one which prevails is the most preferable.

Without a long-term political aim, no present day decision can be rational. But if our strategy is based upon such an aim and if it is a vigilant strategy, we can rid ourselves of the attitude of passivity in face of events evidenced by the anxious question 'What is going to happen?' and substitute for it the active creative question 'What ought we to do?'

Finally, as we have seen, nuclear deterrence perhaps opens up prospects on the nature of things.

The nuclear weapon is one of the products of science. Science has endowed man with powers far exceeding his capacity for foresight and wisdom. Yet in the magnitude of power is inherent its own limitation because of the dangers which go with it. Instead of acquiring wisdom through increased intelligence and a more lively conscience, wisdom is being taught us and forced upon us by material advances capable of bringing us to ruin.

So, as it develops, the world ought to be able to maintain a degree of balance in the fundamental and salutary antithesis between determinism and liberty, between man's power and his freedom of action.